MISSISSIPPI FROM WITHIN

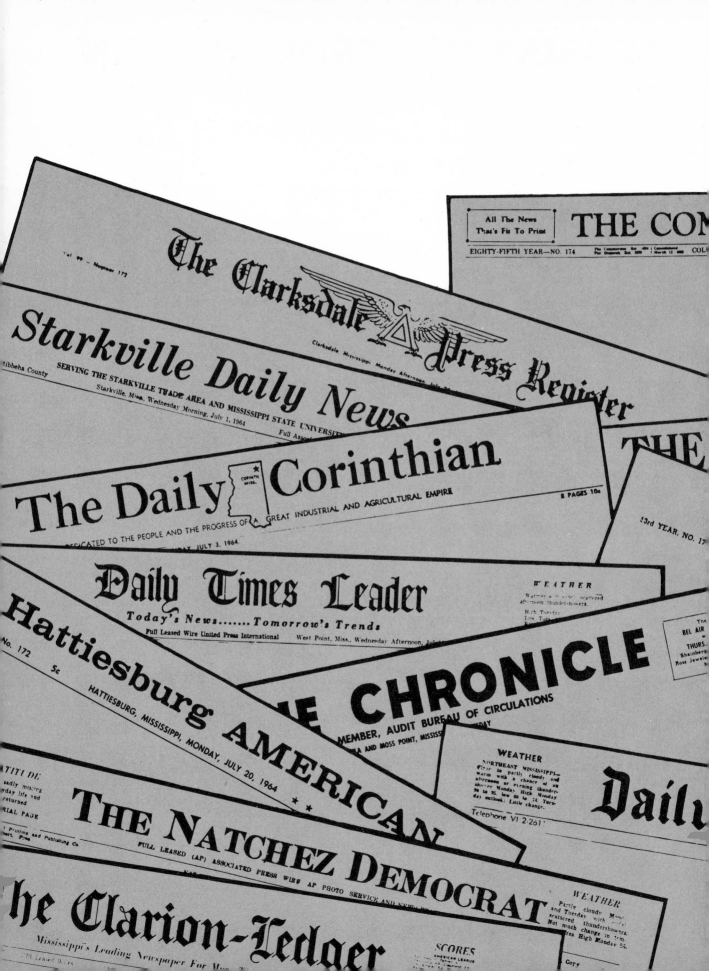

MISSISSIPPI FROM WITHIN

By Shirley Tucker

ARCO PUBLISHING COMPANY, Inc.   New York

Dedication:
To B.W.G.

Published by ARCO PUBLISHING COMPANY, Inc.
219 Park Avenue South, New York, N.Y. 10003

Photo on front cover by Clifford Vaughs

Design by Arthur Ritter, Publishers Art, Inc.

Foreword

MISSISSIPPI FROM WITHIN covers the period from July 2, 1964 (the day the civil rights act was signed into law) to May 1965, when this book went to press. The material comes from over 5,000 issues of Mississippi's 20 daily newspapers — from letters to the editor, news stories, editorials, columns, headlines and advertisements.

An attempt was made to be objective in the selection of material that would show the reaction, attitude and viewpoint of all classes of Mississippians to the civil rights struggle — to integration, segregation, compliance, burnings and bombings, murder, voter registration, and rights workers, to name a few. Space limitations necessitated the cutting and shortening of some of the stories, but in every case a special effort was made to delete only those items that would in no way affect the spirit and meaning of the original. All the material is faithfully reproduced including the errors in capitalization, punctuation and spelling, as well as the occasional omission of a word. In no case was anything added to the original. The only editorializing (if it can indeed be called that) consists of statements clearly marked with a large asterisk, and the photo captions.

No account of this turbulent year would be complete without the graphic evidence of photographs. Although a few have appeared in Mississippi newspapers, most of the photos — often taken under the most hazardous conditions — have never been published.

DE SOTO MARSHALL BENTON TIPPAH ALCORN
TUNICA
TATE
Holly Springs
PRENTISS
TISHOMINGO
PANOLA LAFAYETTE UNION
QUITMAN Oxford LEE ITAWAMBA
COAHOMA Batesville PONTOTOC Tupelo
Clarksdale YALOBUSHA CALHOUN
BOLIVAR TALLAHATCHIE CHICKASAW MONROE
SUNFLOWER Drew GRENADA CLAY
Shaw LE FLORE Grenada WEBSTER West Point
Ruleville CARROLL MONTGOM. LOWNDES
WASHINGTON Greenwood Winona CHOGTAW OKTIBBEHA Columbus
Holly Ridge Indianola Starkville
Greenville HUM. HOLMES ATTALA WINSTON NOXUBEE
SHARKEY
Mileston
ISSAQUENA YAZOO MADISON LEAKE NESHOBA KEMPER
Yazoo City Philadelphia
WARREN HINDS SCOTT NEWTON LAUDERDALE
Vicksburg Tougaloo RANKIN Meridian
Jackson SMITH JASPER CLARKE
CLAIBORNE COPIAH SIMPSON
JEFFERSON COVINGTON JONES WAYNE
LAWRENCE Laurel
ADAMS LINCOLN JEFF. DAVIS
Natchez FRANKLIN Brookhaven LAMAR FORREST PERRY GREENE
WILKINSON AMITE PIKE MARION Hattiesburg
Summit
McComb GEORGE
Magnolia WALTHALL
PEARL RIVER STONE
JACKSON
HANCOCK HARRISON
Biloxi Moss Point
Pascagoula

MISSISSIPPI
Scale of Miles

MISSISSIPPI VOTER REGISTRATION

(1964 Presidential Election)

COUNTY	VOTING AGE POPULATION	NUMBER REGISTERED
SIMPSON		
White	8,073	
Negro	3,186	
SMITH		
White	6,597	
Negro	1,293	
STONE		
White	2,965	
Negro	868	
SUNFLOWER		
White	8,785	7,082
Negro	13,524	185
TALLAHATCHIE		
White	5,099	4,464
Negro	6,483	17
TATE		
White	4,506	
Negro	4,326	
TIPPAH		
White	7,513	
Negro	1,281	
TISHOMINGO		
Wihte	8,068	
Negro	359	
TUNICA		
White	2,011	1,407
Negro	5,822	38
UNION		
White	9,512	
Negro	1,626	
WALTHALL		
White	4,536	4,536
Negro	2,490	4
WARREN		
White	13,530	11,654
Negro	10,726	2,433
WASHINGTON		
White	19,837	
Negro	20,619	
WAYNE		
White	5,881	
Negro	2,556	
WEBSTER		
White	4,993	
Negro	1,174	
WILKINSON		
White	2,340	
Negro	4,120	
WINSTON		
White	6,808	
Negro	3,611	
YALOBUSHA		
White	4,572	
Negro	2,441	
YAZOO		
White	7,598	
Negro	8,719	
ADAMS		
White	10,888	
Negro	9,340	
ALCORN		
White	13,347	
Negro	1,756	
AMITE		
White	4,449	
Negro	3,560	
ATTALA		
White	7,522	
Negro	4,262	
BENTON		
White	2,514	2,226
Negro	1,419	55
BOLIVAR		
White	10,031	
Negro	15,939	
CALHOUN		
White	7,188	
Negro	1,767	
CARROLL		
White	2,969	
Negro	2,704	
CHICKASAW		
White	6,388	4,548
Negro	3,054	1
CHOCTAW		
White	3,728	
Negro	1,105	
CLAIBORNE		
White	1,688	1,528
Negro	3,969	26
CLARKE		
White	6,072	4,829
Negro	2,988	64
CLAY		
White	5,547	
Negro	4,444	
COAHOMA		
White	8,708	
Negro	14,604	
COPIAH		
White	8,153	7,533
Negro	6,407	25
COVINGTON		
White	5,329	
Negro	2,032	
DeSOTO		
White	5,338	
Negro	6,246	
FORREST		
White	22,431	13,253
Negro	7,495	236
FRANKLIN		
White	3,403	
Negro	1,842	
GEORGE		
White	5,276	4,200
Negro	580	14
GREENE		
White	3,518	
Negro	859	
GRENADA		
White	5,792	
Negro	4,323	
HANCOCK		
White	6,813	
Negro	1,129	
HARRISON		
White	55,094	
Negro	9,670	
HINDS		
White	67,836	62,410
Negro	36,138	5,616
HOLMES		
White	4,773	4,800
Negro	8,757	20
HUMPHREYS		
White	3,344	2,538
Negro	5,561	0
ISSAQUENA		
White	640	640
Negro	1,081	5
ITAWAMBA		
White	8,523	
Negro	463	
JACKSON		
White	24,447	
Negro	5,133	
JASPER		
White	5,327	4,500
Negro	3,675	10
JEFFERSON		
White	1,666	
Negro	3,540	
JEFFERSON DAVIS		
White	3,629	3,236
Negro	3,222	126
JONES		
White	25,943	
Negro	7,427	
KEMPER		
White	3,113	
Negro	3,221	
LAFAYETTE		
White	8,074	
Negro	3,239	
LAMAR		
White	6,489	5,752
Negro	1,071	0
LAUDERDALE		
White	27,806	18,000
Negro	11,924	1,700
LAWRENCE		
White	3,878	
Negro	1,720	
LEAKE		
White	6,754	6,000
Negro	3,397	220
(93.6% Negro)		
LEE		
White	18,709	
Negro	5,130	
LEFLORE		
White	10,274	7,348
Negro	13,567	281
LINCOLN		
White	11,072	
Negro	3,913	
LOWNDES		
White	16,460	8,687
Negro	8,362	99
MADISON		
White	5,622	6,256
Negro	10,366	218
MARION		
White	8,997	10,123
Negro	8,630	383
MARSHALL		
White	4,342	4,229
Negro	7,168	177
MONROE		
White	13,426	
Negro	5,610	
MONTGOMERY		
White	4,700	
Negro	2,627	
NESHOBA		
White	9,143	
Negro	2,565	
(79.4% Negro)		
NEWTON		
White	8,014	
Negro	3,018	
(94.2% Negro)		
NOXUBEE		
White	2,997	
Negro	5,172	
OKTIBBEHA		
Wihte	8,423	4,413
Negro	4,952	128
PANOLA		
White	7,639	5,922
Negro	7,250	878
PEARL RIVER		
White	9,765	
Negro	2,473	
PERRY		
White	3,515	
Negro	1,140	
PIKE		
White	12,163	
Negro	6,936	
PONTOTOC		
White	8,772	
Negro	1,519	
PRENTISS		
White	9,535	
Negro	1,070	
QUITMAN		
White	4,176	
Negro	5,673	
RANKIN		
White	13,246	
Negro	6,944	
SCOTT		
White	7,742	5,400
Negro	3,752	16
SHARKEY		
White	1,882	
Negro	3,152	

NOTE: No official figures are available for many of the counties in the NUMBER REGISTERED column.

STATEWIDE FIGURES

COUNTY	VOTING AGE POPULATION	NUMBER REGISTERED
Total by Color		
White	748,266	525,000
Negro	422,256	28,500

LBJ signs the CR bill

Grenada Sentinel-Star, July 3

President leaves Washington quickly

✳ On July 2, 1964 President Johnson signed
the Civil Rights Bill — a law
that had special impact on the slightly
over one million white and
slightly under one million Negro residents
of the state of Mississippi

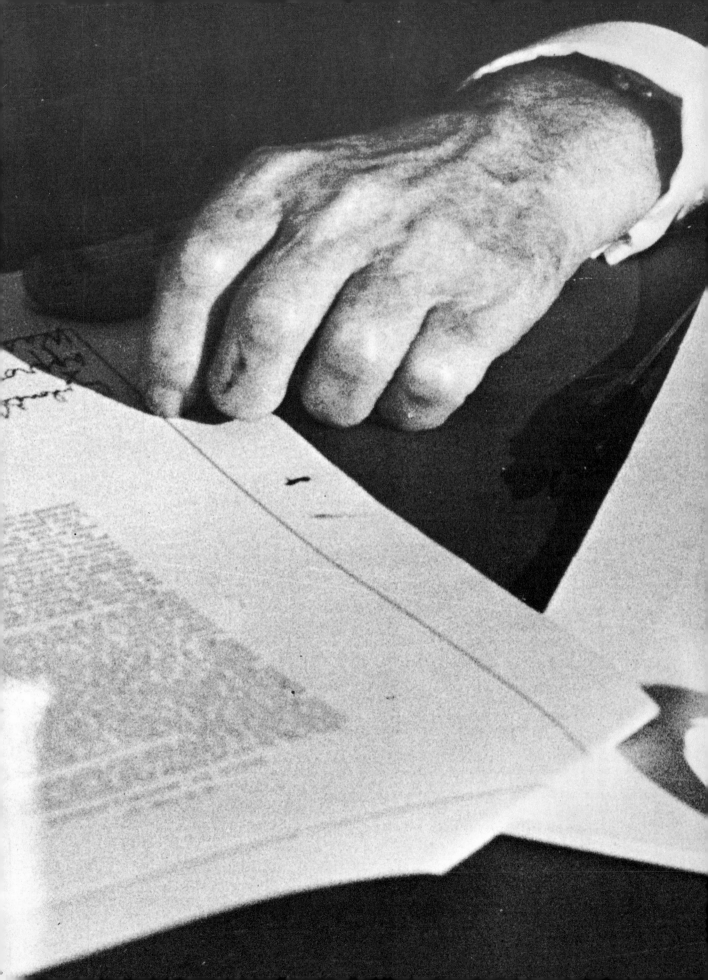

'MISSISSIPPIANS NOT GOING TO BE RUN OVER'

Columbus **Commercial Dispatch,** Aug. 13

Leaflets Dropped On Coast

"The b l a c k savages have threatened that they intend to turn the Gulf Coast into the Congo Coast on the Fourth of July," the leaflet said.

"We are hereby advising all white persons who are not members of duly authorized police forces . . . to stand back and to avoid conflict . . . These people want Mississippi placed under martial law . . .

"Remember that the blacks cannot accomplish anything unless they can cause a disturbance."

There have been no announcements by civil rights leaders in the state of turning "the Gulf Coast into the Congo Coast" on Saturday.

Jackson **Clarion-Ledger,** July 4

THE PEOPLE SPEAK:

Protect Our Rights And The Innocent

MERIDIAN STAR: H e a v e n Help Us Protect Our Rights!

I, among many, many others who disapprove, am in the midst of this Civil Rights conglomeration.

The Negroes were given a native land, the "Congo". Although I admit all races, colors and creeds need an education of some description, why can't they get it in a world of their own and take some of their leaders with them and use the money that is being spent to tour the whole country and cause trouble?

Why doesn't someone take it on himself and organize a committee to load t h e m all into paddy wagons or flat bed trailors and transport them back to their original home and make this a safer place for everyone?

Heaven help us protect our rights and my God protect the innocent. Y o u r s truly, MRS. L.M.H.

Meridian Star, July 21

UPI

Governor advises citizens not to comply with law until tested

Hattiesburg American, July 3

This is one of the saddest Independence Days in the history of our country.

Meridian Star, July 4

July 2, 1964 is another day that will live in infamy.

Pascagoula-Moss Point
Chronicle, July 6

"Integration is like prohibition," Johnson explained, "if people don't want it a whole army can't enforce it. People who want to ensure integration in Mississippi had better think 900,000 times."

Jackson Clarion-Ledger, Aug. 12

"Mississippi must outmaneuver those who would destroy us and our way of life," he said.

Clarksdale Press Register, Aug. 3

Within the next few weeks our governor's actions will echo this slogan, "Stand Tall with Paul," or they will say, "Sit Small With Paul."

Tupelo Journal, July 16

✱ There were those who said, "No!"

The Real American Approach

Regardless of how sincerely we may believe provisions in it to be unconstitutional, the civil rights bill has become, and is now, the law.

Laurel Leader-Call, July 20

For the first time in the past decade, the phrase "law of the land" can be applied. Though we do not like it, and we must do everything in our power, legally, to get it repealed, we have an obligation, as citizens, to respect the law, no matter how utterly distasteful it is.

Vicksburg Post, July 12

If Mississippi is to repair its tarnished 'image' it must prove that its citizens are able and willing to live within the law, and it is to this end that every citizen and every responsible organization should devote itself during "The Long, Hot Summer.'

Delta Democrat-Times, July 13

"The citizens of Jackson have earned a reputation as a law abiding community, and the business and professional leadership of the city, and our elected city officials, have always encouraged all of our people of both races to abide by the law of the land. We may not be in sympathy with all of the laws of the land, but we must maintain our standing as a community which abides by the law."

Jackson Chamber of Commerce,
Hattiesburg American, July 6

✱ **Other Mississippians said, "We don't like it, but it's the law"**

Dear Editor:

Every Northern radical you can find is out to do something for the Negro. The Negro today is the best treated human being in the United States.

It seems to me that some political party should adopt a civil rights program to protect the white people. We are beginning to need it, because we have to pay the biggest portion of the bill to help take care of the Negroes who are tired of working.

God help this country ! ! !

C. M. C.
Clinton

Jackson Clarion-Ledger, July 6

Dear Editor:

An Open Letter to Mayor Thompson and the Directors of the Jackson Chamber of Commerce:

Dear Sirs:

I am writing to commend you for your stand on the recently enacted Civil Rights legislation. Regardless of your personal persuasions, your pronouncements show tremendous courage and realistic understanding. Your action is the first step in opening a society whose "closed" conditions have lately been so graphically portrayed in a book by Professor James W. Silver and in the latest issue of Newsweek.

Sincerely yours,

L. T.
University, Miss.

Jackson Clarion-Ledger, July 10

Mayor Allen Thompson, Jackson

UPI

Jackson Mayor Urges CR Law Compliance

Corinth **Corinthian**, July 10

JACKSON, Miss. (AP) — Mayor Allen Thompson, an ardent segregationist leader, Thursday urged compliance with the new civil rights act although it makes the city "sick all over."

"I know in my heart that is the thing to do," he added.

McComb **Enterprise-Journal**, July 10

Negroes Gain Ground

In Testing Rights Bill

Corinth **Corinthian**, July 3

News Briefs

NEGRO SERVED HERE

John H. Hobbs of 515 Nelson, a Negro, was served without incident at the Holiday Restaurant on Highway 82 East at about 1:15 p.m. Saturday. Hobbs said, "I walked right in and sat in a booth. A few people looked around, but nobody paid me any real attention. The waitress served me without incident." It was the third time a Negro has been served here since the civil rights bill was signed into law.

Delta Democrat-Times, July 12

Does New Rights Law Affect Dolls?

JACKSON, Miss (AP) — Does the new civil rights law affect dolls?

Passersby stopped with hesitant surprise Saturday and gazed at a new window display of the first "integration" since the bill became law.

Exhibited were Negro and white dolls, intermingled in varying, bright doll outfits, as a special doll sale.

Vicksburg Post, July 13

Meanwhile, four unidentified Negro youths attended a previously all-white movie theater while more than a dozen Negroes in several cars were served at a drive-in cafe for whites. At the drive-in, all four tires on one car were slashed while its Negro passengers were inside.

Meridian Star, July 6

One of two Negro women sitting at an integrated lunch counter in a Jackson bus station was struck by a white man, who disappeared before police arrived. Both women were arrested on charges of disturbing the peace.

Vicksburg Post, July 5

Groups of integrationists registered without incident Tuesday night at a resort facility and three hotels in Harrison County.

The group, in an eight-car caravan, arrived in Biloxi at 11:15 p.m. from Moss Point where they had attended a civil rights rally.

Biloxi-Gulfport **Herald**, July 8

Aaron Henry, president of the National Association for the Advancement of Colored People in Mississippi, and several civil rights workers and their Negro attorneys were served lunch at the University of Mississippi Cafeteria last Wednesday.

One official of the State College Board here admitted that the incident had occurred and that the board of trustees of State Institutions of Higher Learning is looking into the matter.

Jackson **Clarion-Ledger**, Aug. 23

*There was some integration

CLOSED IN DESPAIR
CIVIL RIGHTS BILL
UNCONSTITUTIONAL

UPI

16

Don't Eat Or Sleep At Integrated Places, Mississippians Urged

Meridian Star, July 7

JACKSON, Miss., July 15 — (UPI) —Jackson closed one of its parks today on the complaint of 600 white residents who said it was overrun by Negroes.

"They run through our yards screaming 'I'm free,'" said one white woman who signed a petition asking the city council to close the facility.

Tupelo **Journal**, July 16

JACKSON, Miss. (AP) — Attempting to circumvent the new civil rights law, 13 Mississippi businesses have received charters to operate as private clubs.

Hattiesburg American, Aug. 13

The Temple Theater in Leland was closed yesterday "for repairs" and will remain closed for an indefinite amount of time.

Delta Democrat-Times, July 21

The Kiwanis Club announced today plans to open the former city swimming pool this Sunday under a membership plan.

Greenwood Commonwealth, July 10

More than 20 Negroes climbed off a city bus Tuesday afternoon in protest after a 35-year-old Negro woman who declined to give up her seat was arrested and removed from the bus at Hardy St. and 15th Ave.

Hattiesburg American, Aug. 12

JACKSON, Miss., Oct. 2 (UPI) —A Detroit, Mich., minister said Friday he and five other white clergymen were refused service at a downtown coffee shop by the manager who said he would serve their Negro companion "because I have to."

Tupelo **Journal**, Oct. 3

One Jackson restaurant took down its common "we reserve the right to refuse service to anybody" sign and replaced it with one reading "we reserve the right to refuse service to anyone who does not follow our rules."

A cashier declined to say what the "rules" were.

Tupelo **Journal**, July 6

Dear Editor:

There are several large foundations and corporations who practically support the Negro movements. Should we find out these outfits and all stop buying their products they would sing out of the other side of their mouths. It would hurt a lot of people but we shouldn't be the only ones to feel the wrath of the gods in Washington.

G. C.
Columbus, Miss.

Jackson **Clarion-Ledger**, July 17

JACKSON, Miss., July 7 (UPI) —The Robert E. Lee Hotel, which closed its doors to the public rather than integrate, today offered free rooms to state legislators for the rest of the week.

Tupelo **Journal**, July 8

Dear Editor:

According to News items the Robert E. Lee Hotel has closed its doors rather than bow to the Centralized Government in Washington, D. C. It remains to be seen whether or not the Government will permit this hotel to close, they may be hailed into court for contempt of Congress and forced to continue operations as has been done in schools that have been closed.

Sincerely,
J. B. C.
Meridian, Mississippi

Jackson **Clarion-Ledger**, July 14

✶ There was some resistance to integration

17

THE PEOPLE SPEAK:

Races Can Work Together For Progress

A team of black-and-white Mississippi mules near Hattiesburg, Miss.

Matt Herron

MERIDIAN STAR: Driving up into Kentucky on a visit recently, I passed a wagon pulled by a team of two mules. One of the mules was black and the other white. The white mule was on one side of the wagon tongue and the black mule was on the other side. By pulling together, they were making good progress and moving the loaded wagon toward its destination.

This reminded me of the good progress the white and colored races have made here in the South in time past by working together. The thought occurred to me to wonder what would have happened to the wagon and its load, if the black mule had suddenly decided to step over the wagon tongue and be on the same side with the white mule. That just wouldn't do at all. All progress would have stopped right there!

I hope that this simple illustration will help to show the destructive situation we are now in. E. L. S., RFD 1, Meridian.

Meridian Star, Sept. 24

Personal note to Portera Bros. Turkey Farm: You may have a visit from representatives of the Justice Department soon, regarding violations of the civil rights act. We note that you have not integrated your turkeys. All the white ones are on the west side of Highway 45-W, and all the black ones are on the east side.

West Point **Times Leader**, Oct. 6

Dear Editor:

I wonder how many more in our city and state feel the disgust and nausea that I do at the meek and spineless compliance of a number of businessmen with the so-called Civil Rights act. And let's have no whining excuses about it being the law of the land. There was once a law requiring that everyone bow down to Baal. Remember?

No less deserving of contempt are those who continue to patronize the integrated establishments. Are they so lacking in decency and principle or such slaves to gluttony that they couldn't get up and walk out of a restaurant when they see a Negro being served? Are they ashamed to stand up for their convictions — or perhaps they have no convictions.

As for me and my famly, we may have taken our last vacation. but we will never patronize any hotel, motel, or restaurant that accepts Negroes, even if it means that we will never go anywhere again.

Sincerely,
Mrs. C. H. M.
Jackson 9, Mississippi

Jackson **Clarion-Ledger**, July 21

Dear Editor:

...many attempts have been made in the past to "marry" the races at the point of a gun,

so was the "riots" bill passed, but it has even less chance for success than the attempt called "Reconstruction" 100 years ago. The shotgun squad of our "white brothers" in the White House, Cabinet, Court, Congress, the pulpit etc. don't have the strength, courage or intelligence of their grandparents, and the intended bridegroom has lost the ability to stand up for the wedding—can only stoop, sit or lie, mostly in doorways or in the streets where white counterparts lie with him.

It is significant that most prominent "colored" leaders in the current effort to integrate with the white race are themselves not racially pure. Is it not therefore reasonable to believe that the same probably is true of the "white" leaders?

Jackson **Clarion-Ledger**, July 14

Truly Mississippi has come upon evil days; we have been delivered into the hands of the Philistines.

Some of us may be tempted in the agony of our oppression to give up hope—to yield the struggle.

Yet this we can not—dare not—ever do. It is our sacred obligation to keep up the fight for our precious Southern way of life. We must never rest until this foul pollution of integration is forever banished from our soil.

Down to the end of time our children must be taught to know that integration is evil, and that they must never associate in any way socially with the other race.

Meridian Star, Aug. 24

Dear Editor:

The tear jerkers and liberals in our midst would have us believe that race mixing is good for us. They are as crazy as a loon. The only reason that I am white is because my parents worked at staying white. The only reason my daughter is white is because my wife and I worked at staying white...

So white people if you love your mothers, wives, sweethearts, and daughters quit helping the race mixers. You don't have to harm Negroes, just quit helping them. Do you want your state to be another New York?

J. W. B.
Jackson Miss.

Jackson **Clarion-Ledger**, Oct. 29

* Much of the opposition was very emphatic . . . others took a philosophical position

Senator Theodore G. Bilbo speaks in the county courthouse at Collins, Miss., as he winds up his campaign for the democratic nomination for another term in the U. S. Senate. Bilbo urged that Negroes be prevented from voting in the primary. July 1, 1946.

Mississippi Still Fights
For Bilbo Racial Stand

Jackson **Clarion-Ledger**, July 5

NAACP committee
labels state 'hell'

Hattiesburg American, July 10

By TOM ABERNETHY
Miss. Congressman

Agitators in the civil rights movement, all mature adults, have for months been carefully mapping strategy and tactics for disorder in our State. They gleefully promised for us that which they described as a "long hot summer." This was to be their goal in the campaign of provocation which they planned to carry to extended extreme.

Having become filthy rich as "rights" leaders, if the agitation stops they are out of business. So they planned the Mississippi Project and contributed all of their brain energy and effort into making the invasion as explosive as possible.

Starkville News, July 1

Gov. Paul Johnson refused the other day to see a group of Negroes and whites said to be representing minority agitators.

They went down to the first floor of the New Capitol, lined up in front of a bronze statue of the late Sen. Theo G. Bilbo, and read what has been described as an insulting and inflamatory resolution to the unheeding ears of the statue.

A state senator. who had been an admiring supporter of Bilbo for many years and to whom the senator had been a benefactor, strode up in front of the statue, placed his hand in the cold palm of the senator's statue and, we are told, informed the Negro-white integrationists:

"You black SOB. lay a hand on this statue and I will erase you."

A Negro, said to be James Farmer, hesitated, sweat popped from his face at the urging of another Negro, Farmer then read on and the group left hurriedly as a white woman watching from a second floor balcony of the Capitol peppered the blacks with well-aimed peanuts.

Jackson **Clarion-Ledger**, July 12

Asked by a visiting television man if he would confer with Negro leaders, Johnson asked: "What leaders."

Jackson **Clarion-Ledger**, July 3

The Negro-white group of do-gooders didn't get to see the governor and they didn't disturb Sen. Bilbo.

But, they got the attention of at least one legislator, Rep. Alton Phillips, of Noxubee.

"Did you see that motley crowd around at the governor's office?" Phillips asked.

"Nope, I wasn't around there."

"Well, I did. . .and the question I want to ask," Phillips pursued, "is what are our Jackson policemen doing following that bunch around like lackeys? Up until recently, Jackson had one of the proudest police forces in the nation . . . now, they are assigned as nursemaids to race agitators."

Jackson **Clarion-Ledger**,
July 10

* **Integration leaders came to the state to begin testing civil rights laws**

Danny Lyon

Mark Levy

ALL
WHITE
HELP!

BILL & REX
MOVING SERVICE
226-1999

CALL TODAY!

*The old rules still go . . .

22

Advertisement, **West Point Times Leader**, Sept. 28

Advertisement, Biloxi-Gulfport **Herald**, Nov. 2

Advertisement, Hattiesburg American, Oct. 7

Advertisement, **Hattiesburg American**, Sept. 25

23

Ku Klux Klan Membership Is Rapidly Growing

Meridian Star, July 2

United Klans Meeting Here For August 29

Natchez Democrat, Aug. 18

Former McComb Klansman Claims Disavowal Of KKK

Clarksdale **Press Register**, Nov. 27

So serious has the trend toward violence become that the man known as state head of Mississippi's Ku Klux Klan has quit in concern over where the road is leading.

Tupelo **Journal**, July 22

Oct. 2, 1964

Dear Editor
To All Citizens of Mississippi,

Be it known, as of this wonderful day of Our Lord October 2, 1964, that we in the United Klan of America have no knowledge what-so-ever of the violence which has plagued our State.

Due to the harrassment and intimidation of many of the citizens of our State we urge all citizens to refrain from spreading rumors. You may be involving your husband, your dad, your brother or your closest friend who are working honesttry from the Communist conly and legally to save our counspiracy.

We, in the United Klans of America do not choose to be common men. It is our right to be uncommon if we can. We seek opportunity—not security. We do not wish to be a kept citizen, humbled, dulled, by having the state look after us. We want to take the calculated risk; to dream and to build; to fail or succeed. We refuse to barter incentive for a dole. We prefer the challenge of life to the guaranteed existence; the thrill of fulfillment to the state of calm utopia.

We will not trade freedom for beneficence, nor our dignity for a handout. We will never cower before any master or bend to any threat. It is our heritage to stand erect, proud, and unafraid; to think and act for ourself; enjoy the benefits of our creation, and to face the world boldly and say: —This I have done!

We in the United Klan are men who will stand before a demogogue and damn his treacherous flatteries without winking.

I challenge you to refrain from condemning the one organization which is 100 percent Pro-American, without knowing the truth. Will you help save America?? Once this is accomplished wrongs will be redressed, and right will rule the earth. God help us.

The Klan was yesterday, is today and will forever be opposed to Communism in any form. We will fight to our last breath, using every means at our disposal to rid our country of this insidious plague of mankind.

For God and Country,
E. L. McDaniel,
Grand Dragon
Realm of Mississippi

Natchez Democrat, Oct. 10

Fair Image

The Ku Klux Klan has a booth at the Alabama State Fair, complete with a tin foil cross lighted with red bulbs to simulate flames.

Anxious for a better public image after having so many of their members arrested on a variety of charges, the KKK has erected the booth so that citizens can see what a friendly organization it has become.

The Klan vows that it has abandoned violence, even though several of its members have recently been arrested with enough arms and explosives to invade China.

It is pleasant to know that the KKK has changed its ways and become a respectable enough organization to exhibit at a state fair. With such exhibits as neon lighted night riders, the public may soon forget that a few years ago the grand dragon of the KKK was convicted of kidnapping, raping and torturing his own secretary to the point where she committed suicide. Of course, all that has changed, even if a few of the fellows involved in the crime are still members.

We should not be too harsh on the Klansmen. Perhaps in a few years their fair exhibit will include games such as lynch-the-kupie doll, or bomb-the-church. As prizes they can award tiny crosses, which will burst into flames after the winner gets them home—burning his house down.

Delta Democrat-Times, Oct. 9

Brother Sid Harris passes along this thoughtful paragraph in the Houston Times-Post: You will recall that both political parties discussed extremism at great length, whether to indict such organizations as the Ku Klux Klan and the John Birch Society which were labeled "extremists". And yet, a pamphlet passed on to us describes Jesus Christ as the "greatest extremist of all time". When Christ spoke he used no "ifs, ands or buts", but spoke in commands, using such words as "you shall", "you must" and he said "I am the way".

West Point **Times Leader**,
Sept. 10

✳ With the passage of the civil rights bill the white supremist groups in Mississippi became active: "talking and acting," according to their leaders, "in a non-violent way"

Citizens Council Has 'Dial For Truth'

JACKSON, Miss., Aug. 19 — (UPI) — Pick up the telephone and dial 948-5511 here day or night and you hear a recorded voice say:

"This is dial for truth, the 24-hour-a-day service of your Jackson Citizens' Council, with important information for every white resident of the Jackson area."

"Every time there is a (racial) crisis, our normal communications are jammed with people calling in to find out what is going on and what they can do," Morphew said in an interview.

The recorded messages, changed frequently, have run the gamut from criticizing Jackson Mayor Allen Thompson for urging compliance with the civil rights act of 1964 to pleas for letting local law enforcement officers handle racial problems.

The message lasts from about one to two minutes. Morphew views the telephone device as a public service.

Richard Morphew, public relations director, Tupelo **Journal,** Aug. 20

The City Council urgently appeals to the parents of all children to keep them away from dangerous situations created by the Civil Rights Act.

Greenwood Commonwealth, July 14

Dear Tom:

The following notice is now being placed on cash registers and in the windows of many restaurants and other establishments throughout the South.

"Every Penny of Negro Trade Forced on This Establishment Will Be Donated To The Citizens' Council."

I thought you might be interested in this information, Tom.

Sincerely,
Robert B. Patterson
Secretary
Citizens' Council
Greenwood, Miss.

Jackson **Clarion-Ledger,** Aug. 21

New York Times

CITIZENS COUNCIL THEORY:

'No Schooling Better Than Integrated Education'

Tupelo **Journal,** Aug. 24

Barnett Says To 'Organize'

BATON ROUGE (AP) — Ross Barnett, a former governor of Mississippi, told the Citizens Council here the way to maintain racial segregation is to organize.

"Organize," he told the council Tuesday night, "and you can accomplish anything."

Laurel Leader-Call, Oct. 28

Boycott Of Integrated Firms Is Asked By Citizens Council

Jackson **Daily News,** July 9

Jackson Attorney Fires Open Letter To Citizens Council

Howard E. Ross Jr., of Jackson and Clinton, emphasized that he is a Mississippian, a segregationist, and an opponent of the civil rights bill.

If our restaurant had difficulties wrestling with the CR bill before, you have compounded them by your nine point program of ostracism and boycott.

Your ideas of constitutional law as expressed in your nine points is interesting. You may be right. However, I am not going to wait in jail or bankruptcy court until you have had the opportunity to test this theory.

The insurance company holding the mortgage on the restaurateur's home, the bank that has the 90 day notes, and the finance company that has extended credit in order that the innkeeper may drive an automobile will probably not be overjoyed that the Citizens' Council has driven their customer into bankruptcy.

If your executive committee presumes itself to be above the law then please let it operate my restaurant. Frankly, I am not paramount to Acts of Congress, no matter how ardently my wishes might be in that area.

You say repeal the law. We agree this is the approach for all of us. The Congress meets in Washington, however, not in restaurants and hotels in Jackson.

As a substitute for segregation through improverishment let me suggest you consider the following as being an effective means of combatting integration:

1. Vote
2. Write your Congressman
3. Provide financial assistance to groups advocating and working toward repeal.
4. Let the law take its course.
5. Keep calm.
6. Let's hang together.

Jackson **Daily News,** July 9

On the political front, we intend to prevent Negro political domination by uniting the power of white Southerners.

Meridian Star, Oct. 17

"Insofar as my relationship with the Citizens Council is concerned, I have enjoyed a close working relationship with this group and found its leadership equally dedicated to the preservation of law and order in this state.

Gov. Paul Johnson, McComb
Enterprise-Journal, July 2

The councils objected to being referred to as "White Citizens Councils." Reynolds said his group has one Mexican American member.

"They are sweet, wonderful people," he said, referring to his members.

"You should see some of the letters I get. Why, the things they say are so moving, if you read some of them, it would bring tears to your eyes."

Clyde Reynolds, Pres.,
Los Angeles chapter, Jackson
Clarion-Ledger, Aug. 23

"The Jackson chapter built up a card file containing the racial views of nearly every white person in the city," the author says. He goes on to quote an "astute observer" that the Council had, by 1959, "created a climate of fear that has strait-jacketed the white community."

Aligned with the election of Ross Barnett, the Council felt strong enough to list as subversive: the Red Cross, FBI, B.P.O.E., Jewish War Veterans, Methodist Church, and YWCA, to name a few, Silver continues.

Clarksdale Press Register, July 30

MERIDIAN STAR: In regard to Mr. Dulles report to President Johnson on the situation here in Mississippi: He advocated t h e abolishment of several of o u r organizations s u c h as Citizens Council, F r e e d o m for White People. He never said anything about the activities of the Communist led NAACP, Core and others.

It is my humble opinion, that the biggest menace to our freedom at the present is the Federal Courts of the land and our present Administration w h i c h is against everything the S o u t h stands for. Thank you.

Meridian Star, July 9

✱The respectable supremist group is the White Citizens Council. The organization urges civil rights act resistance: "We simply channel the white dollar to the white man"

27

Preserves White Race

Biloxi-Gulfport **Herald**, July 6

APWR President Says His Group Not Violent

McComb **Enterprise-Journal**, July 6

SUMMIT, Miss. (AP) —What sort of an organization is the Americans for Preservation of the White Race?

Its president, W. Arsene Dick, maintains his young segregationist organization is neither secret nor violent, and is not associated with the Ku Klux Klan.

"This organization, as far as I am concerned, is non-political, non-profit, and by all means non-violent."

"We are not merged with anybody," he said. "We are an organization to ourselves, operating in the public according to the by-laws, with members of the male Caucasian race only."

The APWR was formed by nine men in a Natchez service station garage on May 13, 1963.

"If I thought for a minute this was a clandestine organization, I'd get out," Dick said.

Dick, a Navy veteran of World War II, says he came to deeper religious convictions later in life and finds the subject vital to his project.

"They took God Almighty out of everything and that's our trouble today," he said.

McComb **Enterprise-Journal**, July 6

Americans For The Preservation Of The White Race, Inc., advocates: The only means that peaceful co-existence can be attained is by each race and by North and South understanding each other's problems; each having PRIDE in his own race traditions, and home State, and each having RESPECT for the other's feelings, position, and State.

Natchez Democrat, July 9

APWR Will Hear Rev. Nolan Today

Natchez Democrat, Oct. 5

Reverend Nolan will speak on the subject "segregation is Christian Doctrine," using the Bible as his source and background.

All of these addresses by conservative - thinking, noted speakers are being sponsored by APWR in the best interests of the public in line with the policies of APWR inpresenting Truth to the people and have been well - received.

Natchez Democrat, Oct. 5

The True Image

Various groups of racial extremists have suddenly felt the need for a better public image.

One of these groups, which suddenly wants the world to know that it is against all violence, is the Americans for the Preservation of the White Race (APWR).

The truth is not shown in deeds, however. Attending a meeting of APWR, the visitor hears several hours of straight and unwatered hate preached. Hate is preached against Negroes, outsiders, progress, Democrats in Washington, Republicans in Washington, the United Nations, the Catholics, Jews, NATO, SEATO, Congress and assorted other institutions.

According to the "non-political speakers at the APWR meetings, the Communists have taken over the Justice Department, the Supreme Court and the office of the President. About the only place that the Reds have not been successful appears to be Mississippi.

The APWR, which says it seeks to preserve a race, which has somehow managed to preserve itself for several centuries, makes many of the same assumptions that the Nazis made.

Jews, Catholics and people of non-American origin are excluded from the APWR's members and, we assume, from preservation. The non-violent membership gladly takes well known KKK members into it's ranks. Indeed, so many KKK members belong to the APWR in certain areas of southwest Mississippi, that it is impossible to tell tell where one stops and the other begins.

The ironic thing about Hitler s claims and to a like extent, the APWR's protestations, is that both groups probably believe their own press releases.

The APWR has no link with the FBI to run security checks on new members. Hate is the only real qualification.

Delta Democrat-Times, Aug. 8

The local chapter of the Americans for the Preservation of the White Race accused the Jackson Chamber of Commerce Tuesday of bowing to "radical pressure groups and Washington politicians" in calling for obedience to the civil rights act.

"There can now be little doubt that these men have sold the people of Jackson out to radical pressure groups and Washington politicians for selfish profit motives," the APWR said.

The APWR said "Mississippians should know the "officials did not speak for the citizens of Jackson or for the majority of members of their organizations.

Jackson Clarion-Ledger, July 8

APWR officials believe that Mississippi is the ultimate target of the communists because the state had "rejected all communistic tendencies."

McComb Enterprise-Journal, Aug. 4

Former CIA director Allen Dulles, who visited this state two weeks ago as a presidential trouble-shooter, reported "terroristic activity" in Mississippi and called for a crackdown on "clandestine g r o u p s in the state."

Dulles mentioned the Ku Klux Klan and the APWR.

McComb Enterprise-Journal, July 6

* **The newest organization, Americans for the Preservation of the White Race, Inc., was born in an alley garage in Natchez. W. Arsene Dick, president of APWR, said he "came to deeper religious convictions later in life" and finds the subject vital to his project**

CR Invasion Planned To Stimulate Trouble

Starkville News, July 21

'Scared' N. Y. Teachers On Way To Mississippi

Tupelo **Journal**, July 1

The Rev. Mr. Allen expected to encounter hostility. But the instructions he received from National Council of Churches representatives upon his arrival in Mississippi surprised even him.

"We were instructed never to go anywhere alone. Only in real necessity to go out after dark — and then only in a large group or convoy. We should have lock gas tank caps for our car. Hide the car when not in use to protect our tires from being slashed. Keep it always locked so liquor bottles could not be placed in it, thus warranting an arrest for possession of alcoholic beverages.

"We were to disconnect the dome-light of our car so that we would not be silhouetted at night. Never sit in a lighted room without the shades drawn. Sleep as far from the entrance of your dwelling as possible to diminish bomb damage to our persons.

"We were shown how to fall and cover ourselves so we would suffer least damage from being kicked or slugged. We were shown how to fall on top of our friends if he was being beaten too badly. We were told never to fight back — except in one instance. We were to resist with all our strength if they tried to release us from jail after dark, because that would be our death warrant."

Rev. Thomas B. Allen. rector, Episcopal church, Washington, D.C., Grenada **Sentinel-Star**, Aug. 21

* To help break the pattern of segregation, nearly 1,000 students, doctors, ministers and lawyers went to Mississippi in the summer of 1964. The Council of Federated Organization, COFO, coordinated the Mississippi Project. Mississippians reacted in various ways

Ted Polumbaum

Dear Editor.

I am not much of a writter but I am getting to be one mad Yankee. I have lived in your state for just about a year in Yazoo City. Never in my life have I been treated better. I have lived here long enough that I believe that I know the people of both races. I can not understand why the people of the North tolerate this T-shirt gang coming into the South.

Just 100 years ago this nation was fighting a great war for principle on both sides. To try and save a great Nation. I really believe that the great soldiers of that War Robert E. Lee, U. S. Grant, Stonewall Jackson, Phil Sheridan and all the soldiers of both sides would turn over in their graves to see what a mess we have got this nation in. We did not pay enough attention when Hilter had his little gang of Brown Shirts and Mussolini had his gang of Black Shirts and now today under the present administration the gang of the dirty T Shirt.

A Mad Yankee
From Yazoo City.

Jackson **Clarion-Ledger**, July 3

MERIDIAN STAR: Open letter to all Negroes in Mississippi:

If I were a Mississippi Negro I would personally meet the next bus load of these invaders and send them back to the slum areas of the Northern cities that they came from. Judging by the personal appearance of the ones that I have seen, I would say that they have just crawled from beneath a garbage can just long enough to come to Mississippi to teach you betterment for yourself.

The next one of them, white or black that you see, ask him to show you at least $5.00 that he has actually worked for. Also, ask them if they have a gainful **trade** to teach you. D C.

Route 3

Meridian Star, July 16

Rights Workers Urged to Register With Police

McComb **Enterprise-Journal**, July 1

Gov. Johnson said the northern college students who poured into the state this summer for civil rights activities were an "outside, broken down, motley bunch of atheists."

Corinth **Corinthian**, Sept. 24

He said the Mississippi Negroes had turned "the back of their hands" to what he called a "motley crowd of first generation aliens" in the "summer project" in the state. "We appreciate that the Negroes in Mississippi have stood with us in these troubled times," Johnson said.

Gov. Paul Johnson, **Meridian Star**, Aug. 13

Ross Suggests Righters Bathe

McComb **Enterprise-Journal**, July 5

"White Mississippians for the most part just look at these backward children, shake their heads and laugh," said Ross Robert Barnett, the former governor in appraising the project.

"If these wandering minstrels would simply go home, take a bath, shave and put on a clean pair of socks then I know that Mississippi would be better off. I can't help but think these backward children would be better off, too."

Delta Democrat-Times, July 28

"As a matter of fact, these traveling agitators have been calling Washington every day, saying they need some federal marshals around them to make them feel safe. But I say why be half safe? Why send a couple of carloads of marshals to look after them when a couple of cases of Mister Clean would do a lot more good?

"If you folks haven't seen any of these people, you don't know what you're missing' The boys have such long hair — and the girls have such short hair — that it's hard to tell them apart. They talk through their noses. And the clothes they're wearing make me think that the scarecrows on my farm in Madison county, Mississippi, have started dressing for dinner'

Ex-Governor Ross Barnett, Jackson **Clarion-Ledger**, July 6

Dear Editor:

We may call them names, accuse them of "invasion"; we may send them away in disgust with Mississippi's "closed mind" and in fear of brutal treatment, or we may meet them halfway, get acquainted, show them what to us is the real Mississippi — our schools and colleges for both races, our industries, historical treasures, records of struggle and achievement in education, finance, and religion, and introduce them to leading citizens who can give them the information they need.

yours sincerely.
An Old Subscriber

Jackson **Clarion-Ledger**, July 29

"Some folks in Mississippi are even carrying a little mirror around in their pockets so that if they happen to see one of these strange characters they just invite him to take a look at himself and see if he looks like the rest of the people in the community."

Jackson **Clarion-Ledger**, July 3

Steve Schapiro

COFO civil rights worker arriving in Canton, Miss., where he helped to enlist Negroes to vote.

Negro paper asks workers to go home

Hattiesburg American,
July 21

Many of the "wholesome young Americans" who are in Mississippi to help "educate" a portion of our population can be described in this fashion: Wearing blue jeans, sweat shirts, tennis shoes, badly in need of a haircut, perhaps with a young fuzzy beard, and carrying a guitar case. Need we say more?

West Point **Times Leader**, July 1

The student volunteers—the beatniks, the wild-eyed left wing nuts, the unshaven and unwashed trash, and the just plain stupid or ignorant or misled — go on meddling and muddling with things about which they know nothing and which concern them not.

Meridian Star, July 12

✱ The initial group of 175 volunteers arrived in the state June 20 and began working on voter registration — canvassing neighborhoods and holding voter registration classes

Baptist pastor questions motives

I am personally convinced that what is going on here involves more than the civil-rights issue, and that it is sinister and dangerous beyond anything we have yet supposed.

Rev. Eldie F. Hicks, First Baptist Church, Waynesboro, **Hattiesburg American**, July 28

Johnson urged Mississippians to stand shoulder to shoulder in what he called "a time of testing." "If we are divided in any way, we all suffer," he said.

He reaffirmed a previous stand that "we are not going to allow a group of outsiders to come in and drive a wedge into the unity of this state."

Clarksdale Press Register, Aug. 3

The state's difficulties cannot be solved by accusing 'outsiders' of coming in "to drive a wedge into the unity of the state," as Johnson charged.

As long as we continue to blame others for difficulties that are essentially of our own making, we can no more expect the difficulties to end than can a laggard student who persists in blaming an 'unfair' teacher expect to raise his grades without cracking a book.

Delta Democrat-Times, Aug. 14

The underlying aim of the "citizenship" curriculum, a COFO worker says is to teach the Mississippi Negro "to question — to question the written word, to question the radio, not to believe everything heard."

Biloxi-Gulfport **Herald,** July 10

"I believe that the program is a constructive one. The basic elements of voter registration, community centers and freedom schools is the kind of program that can help develop not only the Negro community but also the total community.

Rev. Richard Rowe, campus minister, Stanford University, **Delta Democrat-Times,** July 13

"We are seeking desperately to establish a medium of communication between the white and colored races here," said the Rev. Alfred R. Winham, pastor of Grace Church of Christ in Holyoke.

"When one man has not got equal rights, then no man has equal rights," explained Mrs. Winham.

"As Christians we believe in living our religion not just for the future, but in the present."

Tupelo Journal, July 10

Negro Group Organizes Anti-COFO Unit In MP

A Mississippi Negro group moved into Moss Point Wednesday to oppose work carried on there by integrationist organizations.

With the "wholehearted" support of Sheriff Cecil Byrd, the Negroes will pass out pamphlets, talk to older people and solicit help in appealing to younger Negroes.

Gillespie said his group is non-profit and accepts no donations "from the Citizens Council or any other organization," but receives some support from private citizens.

Pascagoula-Moss Point **Chronicle,** July 6

JACKSON (UPI) — Two U.S. congressmen expressed admiration Sunday for the "responsible and mature" actions of student volunteers in a massive civil rights drive in Mississippi.

Reps. Philip Burton, D-Calif., and William Fitts Ryan, D-N.Y., departed for their homes following a weekend tour of the state.

Ryan said he was departing convinced "the Negro citizen in Mississippi who wants to vote and to take part in the normal life of the community lives in fear and terror.

"Harassment and intimidation are his daily bread," he said.

West Point **Times Leader,** July 6

and qualities of 'freedom workers'

Hattiesburg American, July 28

Ted Polumbaum

Moods and faces
of civil rights workers
in Mississippi, summer, 1964

Steve Schapiro

Ted Polumbaum

Ted Polumbaum

COFO workers arrive at Meridian, Miss.

* The volunteers, who lived with
Negro families, received no
pay. They were told to be
prepared to furnish their own
bond money if arrested

***Faces and Moods
of civil rights workers
in Mississippi**

summer, 1964

Herbert Randall

Peter Cummings

Herbert Randall

Ted Polumbaum

Robert Fletcher

Civil rights workers arrival at Canton, Miss.

*Another group came later to organize "freedom schools," instructing Negroes in academic subjects and citizenship.
Some Mississippians said there was too much freedom

Dear Editor:

According to the news reports, the "Freedom Houses" set up in Mississippi by the National Council of Churches, assures to its civil rights workers the ultimate freedom of choice. An explosion wrecked a ROOM, in a Negro's home in which a mixed group of 10 civil rights workers slept, in McComb, with different sexes and colors. You can't beat that for freedom, but I can't say how much bravery was involved.

As Mr. Taliaferro says, "this may not be in good taste," but I think the reason some of the white clergy in Mississippi, defend the National Council of Churches, (with vigah), is because they hope to get an invitation to "freedom house."

Jackson **Clarion-Ledger**, July 21

Dear Editor:

What I have seen of the COFO workers they are of low moral character. I have written proof of the number of these workers who are pregnant and unmarried. I also have a documented file of places where the white boys and Negro girls have lived together illegally. Is this God's way or is this the way of Satan?

Jackson **Clarion-Ledger**, Aug. 22

MERIDIAN STAR:

These COFO foreigners are worse than traitors. I am 100% against inter-marriage. I think less of these COFO foreigners than I do of an ant that has been snuffed out.

Meridian Star, Aug. 30

Students' Go Home

Natchez Democrat, July 29

Steve Schapiro

The youngsters were brainwashed to think that they would be making a noble and patriotic mission to help some imaginarily oppressed people.

Anyone with brain no greater than that of a gnat should have understood the hidden motives of the organization heads sponsoring the invasion. As "professionals" of their race and faith, they had a vested interest in what they were sponsoring. They live sumptuously. They have luxury apartments in New York and Washington. They ride in big limousines and chartered planes. They bask in the limelight and adulation of leading liberals, big church leaders and the big politicians up to the level of the White House, which frequently flatters them with a summons for counsel and advice.

By Congressman Abernethy,
Starkville News, July 1

"I went to Mississippi," he says, "because there is injustice there. If this can happen in one corner of this land, it can happen in every corner."

Does he really feel that he did any good for the Negroes in Mississippi — or did the summer influx of outside civil rights workers perhaps make their lot even harder?

"I asked that question of nearly every Negro to whom I talked. The answer was always about the same. 'Things will be bad when you leave. But we needed your help to stand up straight. We're glad you came.'

Rev. Thomas B. Allen, rector, Episcopal church, Washington, D.C., **Delta Democrat-Times**, Aug. 20

Clifford Vaughs, SNCC

Steve Schapiro

It was set on fire in the middle of a heavily timbered swamp.

You don't fool around with fire under those circumstances — not if its your own home that's threatened.

So for that reason alone, it's obvious that scores of people knew about that burned station wagon long before it was officially discovered.

Pascagoula-Moss Point
Chronicle, July 7

FRIENDLY ADVICE

Perhaps a crude observation is made by old-timers but it makes sense.

"If the three youths were in the area un-alive, the vultures would signal or the waters would lift."

Jackson **Clarion-Ledger**, July 1

Actually, if the three men are alive (and we pray that they are) they're safer in Mississippi than anywhere else on earth! Why? Simply because ALL Mississippians hope they will be found alive. But there are many from other states who are actually hoping that they will be found dead in this state.

West Point **Times Leader**, July 1

MERIDIAN STAR: Currently international attention is focused upon the "Search In Mississippi". From all quarters there is wide-spread speculation about what the determined searchers will find. Will they find a trio of smiling smirchers of this state or will it be a threesome of martyred corpses?

Meridian Star, July 3

There are no more anxious groups of residents crowding street corners. Discussion of the mysterious disappearance is limited to quick questions and occasional jokes.

Vicksburg Post, July 1

The Rev. Roy Collum Jr., pastor of the First Baptist Church, said in an interview in Shreveport, La., that Philadelphia residents resent news reports which represent them as vicious, savage and backward people.

West Point **Times Leader**, July 2

"Philadelphia always has been a peaceful town," the Rev. Roy Collum Jr., pastor of the First Baptist Church, told newsmen. "Even now it is a peaceful town, but there is some tension between the races as neither seems sure of where the other stands."

Starkville News, July 2

✳ On the opening day of the "Mississippi Project" three civil rights workers disappeared. Two days later their burned-out station wagon was found 13 miles northeast of Philadelphia

EASTLAND SAYS
'Missing' Workers Can Be Hoax

Starkville News, July 23

"No one wants to charge that a hoax has been perpetrated, because there is too little evidence to show just what did happen. But as time goes on and the search continues, if some evidence of a crime is not produced. I' think the people of America will be justified in considering other alternatives more valid solutions to the mystery, instead of accepting as true the accusation of the agitators that heinous crime has been committed."

Sen. James O. Eastland (D.),
Tupelo **Journal**, July 23

Sailors Poke Around Swamps For 3 Missing

Biloxi-Gulfport **Herald**, July 1

Steve Schapiro

✱ State troopers, FBI agents and a force of 400 Navy men covered ten predominantly rural counties looking for the three civil rights workers

July 21, 1964
Dear Mr. Editor:

I would like to say a few words of praise on behalf of the poor Navy boys who are having to tramp through the woods and dusty roads in the hot sun. I know that they feel very much out of place. Yesterday a group of about 20 stopped at our door and asked my husband and me for water. We fixed them ice water and they sat and rested in the yard for a few minutes, there was a colored man with them and he was served just as the others were. They all looked like they would have rather been home with their mothers.

A Reader

Neshoba **Democrat**, July 30

Questioned on the three missing COFO workers who disappeared at Philadelphia, Johnson said that they could be anywhere and he would not advance a guess where. He said he had received rumors of their whereabouts from all over the country, but no one had sought to impersonate the three or any one of them.

Gov. Paul Johnson,
Jackson **Clarion-Ledger**, July 3

If this whole thing is by any means a hoax, those three CR workers will turn up sooner or later when they realize they don't matter that much.

Meridian **Star**, July 21

Now about these so - called missing civil rights workers, they are no more missing than I am. They are in a safe place, most likely in a Northern state in a swanky hotel. They dropped out of sight for one reason and that was to get the F. B. I. in our state. Mississippi people are not fools and they don't believe these men met any form of foul play.

Meridian **Star**, July 26

If they were murdered, it is by no means the first case of such disposition by Communists of their dupes to insure their silence. However, the careful absence of clues makes it seem likely that they are quartered in Cuba or another Communist area awaiting their next task. There is no reason to believe them seriously harmed by citizens of the most law-abiding state of the union.

Jackson **Clarion-Ledger**, Aug. 3

Wild stories made the rounds. They had been killed and their bodies slipped into quicksand that prevails in the Bogue Chitta swamp near Philadelphia, said some. They had been fed into the claws of a sawmill "hog," said others.

Jackson **Clarion-Ledger**, Aug. 10

Steve Schapiro

Why The Distinction?

Whatever the announced mission — in this case a search — the presence of the military in Mississippi isn't going to be lost on Mississippians.

"Though the presence of uniformed U. S. militia in Mississippi may be explained officially as for various reasons, the cold fact remains that armed forces are there as the result of Presidential action."

The United States government has lots of FBI men in Mississippi, supplementing first batch sent there. It has more FBI agents scattered around the country it could assign to the State. And, of course, it has literally hosts of other civilian officers it could also put into the search, such as marshals, game wardens, personnel from the border patrol, etc. Yet, it sends members of the military service and, subsequently, reinforcements from the same source.

Is there a reason for the distinction?

Pascagoula-Moss Point **Chronicle**, July 7

* State investigators were "pleased with the progress" of the investigation into the disappearance of the civil rights workers. There wasn't a single clue. "We're stymied," said one officer

Search Goes On, and on

West Point **Times Leader**, July 2

"THIS SEARCH by the Navy for the lost Freedom Riders is ridiculous to the extreme," o p i n e s Lamar Sledge, editor the Kemper County Messenger at DeKalb not far from the big Meridian Naval Air Base, and right next door to world-famous Philadelphia, Miss.

"It is not a search," Sledge complains, "just an aimless, random ride up and down country roads.

"Occasionally a few will walk about 10 or 15 yards off the road and kick over a leaf and say, 'Well, they aren't under there'."

Jackson **Clarion-Ledger**, July 31

Several Negro CORE leaders have made public statements to the effect that they have information that the three missing civil rights workers were killed in Neshoba County near Philadelphia, by a white man. They should either "put up or shut up". Continuing to make such claims, without telling proper authorities the details of the so-called information they supposedly hold, should place them in the position of "withholding information." This deed, in itself, is a violation of the law.

West Point **Times Leader**, July 1

If certain people could forget the long lost CR workers and get the ones on the loose and lock them up, maybe we could soon breathe clean fresh air again. Like many others, I am just an innocent by-stander who eventually will have to suffer the consequences more so than now. Id like mighty well to see "Old Glory" continue to wave proving our liberty, freedom and justice to all. As it appears now, there isn't much of either for anyone.

Meridian Star, July 21

So the big Philadelphia show goes on — people and news printing trash about our nice Americans in the Philadelphia area and the state of Mississippi. All of it for one purpose and one only — Lyndon Johnson wants to be re-elected President of the United States. When and if he thinks he has the Negro vote he will stop all this useless searching.

America and its people will profit nothing by this civil rights bill either. Maybe Johnson will, but the people will not. Everyone knows we can have trouble from it and that is all. Thank you for listening to me. Mrs. R. W., DeKalb, Miss.

Meridian Star, July 21

Steve Schapiro

Some Preacher, This Martin Luther, Says 'Chaplain Of Bourbon Street'

Meridian Star, July 26

Rev. Bob Harrington, known as the "Chaplain of Bourbon Street" in New Orleans, announced plans Saturday here to project the other side of this great state.

"Some preacher, this Martin Luther King. He comes into a community like Philadelphia where people are hungering and thirsting for some good news: instead of a Bible, he uses a cue stick: instead of good news from God, he brought more confusion.

"I challenge Martin Luther King to explain his authority to call himself a minister of the gospel, when the gospel is the good news of the Lord to seek and save the lost.

The minister named three things Americans need to know. First, get saved; second, live like it; and third, win others. "This is equality at its best," he concluded.

Neshoba Democrat, July 30

Dear Editor:

For the past sixteen years I've been a faithful reader of the Clarion Ledger, and intend to be for the next sixteen. But, would like to open the paper just one morning and find no mention of Civil Rights, integration, or even segregation.

If you have a paper as far back as a 1953 issue, couldn't you just to break the monotony, run a reprint of the front page?

Mrs. C. J. E.
Oak Forest Drive
Jackson

Jackson **Clarion-Ledger,** July 15

Dear Editor:

God has given our President the courage to put on the headlight of justice and given the Negro the courage to protest peacefully, and some the courage to die. All that wanted to put on the head light of justice and haven't, put it on.

Let it shine and make God's world a better place to live.

Mrs. A. J. N.
West Pearl
Jackson, Miss.

Jackson **Clarion-Ledger,** July 10

King Tells Pool Hall Crowd Trio Are Dead

Jackson **Clarion-Ledger,** July 25

UPI

A low-flying airplane dropped Ku Klux Klan leaflets around a meeting hall at Greenwood Tuesday night while Dr. King was speaking.

"This present mission is no different from any others the 'Riot King' has conducted in the sense that it is designed to bring riot, strife and turmoil to Greenwood," the leaflet said.

"The local Negroes have failed thus far to realize that the 'Riot King' and themselves collectively are today just very black, very ignorant, very dumb and ill smelling . . ."

McComb **Enterprise-Journal,**
July 22

Mississippi Holds Key To Future Of United States, Rev. King Says

Delta Democrat-Times, July 23

The Rev. Ralph Abernathy, secretary of the Southern Christain Leadership Conference which King heads, brought the rally to an emotional pitch with an impassioned speech aimed at rasing funds for the new Freedom Democratic Party.

"I want you to give this movement the price of a good fifth of scotch," Abernathy said. Within a few minutes the audience had contributed $1,288.

Delta Democrat-Times, July 23

The Rev. King, representing the Southern Christian Leadership Conference, arrived in Greenwood by air from Jackson yesterday afternoon to personally canvas for voter registration.

He was received by the the Negro community in Greenwood with wild admiration and he was hailed everywhere he went with displays of emotion.

Delta Democrat-Times, July 22

"Our nation has sent out Peace Corps volunteers throughout the underdeveloped nations of the world and none of them experienced the kind of brutality and savagery" that civil rights workers have experienced in Mississippi, King said at a news conference shortly after his arrival at Jackson from Greenwood.

Delta Democrat-Times, July 23

With A Straight Face

Pascagoula-Moss Point Chronicle, Oct. 18

The Nobel Committee of the Norwegian National Assembly announced with a straight face this week that it had decided to award the Nobel peace prize for 1964 to Martin Luther King, Jr.

Our first reaction to the announcement about King was that it had been made in Norwegian and got garbled in translation.

Pascagoula-Moss Point
Chronicle, Oct. 18

Giving the Nobel peace prize to Martin Luther King is like giving a health certificate to Typhoid Mary.

Starkville News, Oct. 16

Dear Editor:
The Nobel Prize and the Pulitzer Prize are consistently awarded to the radical left. Surely some writer of the right at least knows how to paragraph and punctuate, but they are never recognized.
Sincerely Yours,
S. H. L.
Tupelo

Jackson Clarion-Ledger, Nov. 25

Dear Editor:
First off, I am a Southerner of Tennessee and Mississippi who is retired from the USAF and have been stationed in all areas of the U. S.

Now, could you answer for me a question? According to articles in your newspapers, rabble-rousing King and associates asked his audience to contribute the price of a good bottle of Scotch and it appears that the audience was well aware of the price of good Scotch since the $1288 collected averaged $6.50, per person. How could these people, obviously not working, either know the price or have the money to make such contributions? Was the cash deposited in a local bank to aid local Negroes or did it leave the state?
Maj. C. H. D.
USAF (Ret.)
Jackson, Miss.

Jackson Clarion-Ledger, July 29

* Rev. Martin Luther King's five- day tour of Mississippi took him from pulpits to poolrooms and to nearby Philadelphia, where he told a crowd of about 50 Negroes that the three missing civil rights workers "probably have given their lives for your freedom and my freedom"

J. Edgar Hoover and Governor Paul Johnson

Big Guns Flashed!
FBI Hard To Find?

Vicksburg Post, July 10

Asked if the Federal Bureau of Investigation was helping to defend civil rights, Reed replied:

"That's an interesting question. It's hard to tell who is in the FBI and who isn't. Everyone walks around with a gun and looks evil. The FBI is not protecting people from being murdered."

Eugene Reed, pres., of N.Y. branches, NAACP., Vicksburg Post, July 10

Collins, 33, a big burly man, denied the brutality charges, aired Wednesday night at a mass meeting attended by the NAACP group.

Negroes told the NAACP directors the brutality charges have been turned over to the Department of Justice. Collins said, however, he has not been questioned by either FBI agents or Justice Department attorneys concerning the charges.

"We're friends," Collins said of the FBI agents here. "We have coffee together every day."

Collins described the racial situation here as tense but under control.

Police Chief Ben Collins, Clarksdale, Columbus Commercial Dispatch, July 10

He said he could not agree with Hoover that Sheriffs and deputy sheriffs had participated in crime in some Mississippi areas.

"We have very little trouble in Mississippi in spite of what news media puts out," he said.

Gov. Paul Johnson, Delta Democrat-Times, Nov. 30

NEW ORLEANS (AP) — Two Mississippi highway Patrolmen in the southern area have been fired for being members of the terroristic Ku Klux Klan, it was reported Saturday.

Patrol Chief A. D. Morgan declined comment, except to say: "There are no Klansmen in the Highway Patrol now."

Vicksburg Post, Sept. 27

Hoover Leaves State; Negro Church Burned

Jackson **Clarion-Ledger**, July 12

'Insulted' By FBI

State Sen. Robert Crook, in a speech to the Senate, said the national administration should have sent a senator to check on the racial situation instead of "the cloak and dagger man."

He said several years ago there were 20 agents in Mississippi and "now they have 200 FBI agents . . . carrying out the wishes of Bobby Kennedy. It is just another calculated insult by the administration."

Meridian Star, July 10

✱ J. Edgar Hoover came to Jackson for the opening of an FBI office. He disclosed that an additional 50 men had been assigned to the state. Asked about the civil rights law, Hoover said, "I don't think it's a subject to resolve in the streets"

Before Hoover's plane was in the air, FBI agents already were in Greenwood to investigate the fire at the Pleasant Plains Missionary Baptist Church, which is surrounded by a white subdivision.

Jackson Clarion-Ledger, July 12

To All Mississippians:

We as patriotic Americans do not condone any acts of violence, but honestly believe that the law officers of our great State can handle any acts of violence which may occur without the help of the federal government.

We in the United Klans will use every means at our disposal to rid our country of this and other insidious plagues which we face.

The United Klan is not anti-Catholic, anti-Jew, nor anti-Negro, but 100 percent pro-American!

God help us in this fight. If God is with us who can be against us?

Yours for God and Country
E. L. McDaniel, Grand Dragon
Realm of Mississippi.

P. S.: Why won't the F.B.I. investigate COFO, SNCC, CORE AND the NAACP and leave the patriotic Americans alone?

Jackson Clarion-Ledger,
Sept. 30

"The Federal Bureau of Investigation has just recently called to attention that Mississippi has the lowest crime rate in the country," Barnett said.

"And the FBI has just opened a headquarters with more than 150 men in Jackson at which I have no doubt they intend to train agents in Mississippi law enforcement methods so they can go out over the nation and keep law and order the Mississippi way," Barnett said.

Ex-Gov. Ross Barnett,
Jackson Clarion-Ledger, Aug. 21

Dear Editor:

Mr. "Bay of Pigs" Dulles met with "responsible" leaders of Mississippi and from those meetings decided he should recommend to Billie Sol's Buddy, more FBI participation in the law enforcement affairs of the State of Mississippi.

I have one question to ask! What person or group gave this Potomac Swami the information on which to base his report to LBJ? I don't believe it was our governor, but regardless of who it was I think that this person or persons should come forward.

Mississippi Forever,
A. M. S
Jackson

Jackson Clarion-Ledger, July 6

With so many FBI agents sleuthing in our state we should keep our eyes open and our mouths shut.

J. H. Mc D
Jackson, Miss.

Jackson Daily News, July 7

49

On Being Investigated By The F.B.I.

"Our Washington correspondent writes the following report. In view of the fact that an increasing number of white people are being questioned in Mississippi by F.B.I. Agents, as an outgrowth of the Mississippi Summer Project, and are being harassed to an extent never before known, it is of special importance to give his conclusions:

a. When the FBI agent calls upon you, insist upon complete identification. They carry their credentials (plus a photograph), and you have a right to examine those credentials carefully and in detail. Copy down the name, address, and FBI number of the agent.

b. The FBI agent is supposed to tell you that you are not required to answer his questions. Some agents tell you that, but others do not. If the agent does not make that introductory statement, ask him if you are under a court order to provide information.

c. Say nothing to the FBI agent. When questioned, say "no comment."

d. The FBI agents are given special training in regard to the silent subject who refuses to answer questions. They

---

*In some areas there was strong resistance to FBI activities

Lawyers Advise Citizens of Rights

West Point **Times Leader**,
July 31

It would be good for local citizens to remember that he is not obliged to give any information or answer any questions asked him by Federal officials.

Starkville News, Aug. 21

will try to make you angry, in order that your tongue may be loosened. They will play upon your sympathy ("I don't like this assignment, Mr. - - - - I'm a Southerner, too—but I have been ordered by my Kennedy-appointed superior to question you."), and they will try flattery as well. The best way to defeat such training is to apply the following three rules: (1) silence; (2) more silence; (3) still more silence.

e. Be careful of the FBI man who calls you down to his automobile and opens a conversation with you at that location. There will most certainly be a tape recorder in the car, and your conversation will find its way to Washington via air mail.

f. If meetings are held at your home, someone will check the numbers on the license plates in order to trace the name and address of the individual owner.

g. Your telephone could be tapped, and your house could be "bugged." You can throw a legal monkey wrench into those practices by saying, at a meeting or over the telephone, "If my conversation is being recorded, it is being done so without my permission." By recording that statement, the FBI will be destroying the court value of the "bug." (As you know, a "bug" is a small microphone.)

h. If you are under a court order to provide information to the FBI, you do not have to say anything without first consulting your attorney. In other words, you are entitled to the presence of your attorney before you make a statement.

i. FBI agents are graduates of law schools, i. e., they are lawyers. One of the weak points about the FBI is that its agents can frequently be spotted: A lawyer looks like a lawyer. The FBI uses persons other than lawyers, of course, and those persons frequently infiltrate organizations in order to engage in spy work."

Advertisement, **Meridian Star,** Nov. 8

Natchez, Miss.
November 16, 1964

People's Forum

Concerning the statements made in the above mentioned article, that the FBI had at least sixty informers who have seeped into Klaverns in Mississippi and are feeding back information to the FBI on KKK strategy, plans for dynamiting, schedules of secret meetings and names of the secret leaders, let me point out that these stooges will never send back plans for dynamiting because the Klan in which I am a member does not advocate such terrible acts of violence, nor any acts of violence in any manner. We do not deny that there are stooges getting into the organization, but we know who they are and once they are in, they see for themselves the Klan is not what the news media makes it to be. Therefore, we have a chance to convert these men into Patriotic Americans and true white men. And I cannot recall a one of these men being shot in the back as this article implicates could happen.

If the citizens of Adams County and the State of Mississippi would only Pray before they Preach in condemning the one organization that is fighting for Christian civilization and freedom in America, they would know the truth and the truth would make them free.

God will help those who help themselves. Our prayer is America will come back to God.

Yours for God and Country,
E. L. McDaniel,
Grand Dragon
United Klans of America
Realm of Mississippi

Natchez Democrat, Nov. 18

How Many Murders Undetected in State?

It would be interesting to know just how many murders, suicides and accidental deaths are written off yearly in Mississippi as "death by natural causes";

In Mississippi, about the only requirement for a coroner and ranger, as he is called, is to get elected.

There often are autopsies when a law officer becomes suspicious or when there is obvious foul play. All too often, however, it must be suspected that many secrets are buried along with dead bodies.

McComb **Enterprise-Journal**, Nov. 20

PICKENS, Miss., (UPI)—Authorities said late Wednesday there was no evidence of foul play in the death of a 14-year-old Negro whose body was found in the Big Black River.

"It's simply a case of drowning," said Holmes County Sheriff Andrew P. Smith.

Sheriff Smith discounted reports by civil-righters that the Negro was wearing a CORE T-shirt when he disappeared Monday
Meridian Star, Sept. 10

Holmes County coroner Jay J. Kazar said:

"I l o o k e d him over and couldn't see any bruises around his head or arms," he said. "He apparently choked to death under water."
Laurel Leader-Call, Sept. 10

JACKSON CRIME RATE DOWN 21.8% IN MAY

Jackson **Clarion-Ledger**, July 2

* About a week after Hoover's visit the official "Uniform Crime Reports — 1963," issued by the FBI and the Justice Department, was released, naming Mississippi the state with the lowest crime rate. The state's newspapers gave wide coverage to the report

The governor fell back on Mississipi's standard hallucinatory approach to the state's troubles.

Johnson cited Mississippi's low crime rate and said, in view of the state's large Negro population, "this points out that the segregated life is the peaceful way of life."

Bunk. If Johnson's remark was, in fact, accurate the three civil rights workers bodies would never have been found. In fact, the trio would never have come to Mississippi because there would have been no reason for a militant civil rights movement here.

If the state's low crime rate does indeed indicate 'peace' it certainly does not indicate content.

Delta Democrat-Times, Aug. 14

Mississippi Leading Nation
As Most Law-Abiding State

Jackson **Clarion-Ledger**, July 23

It Is A Fact—We Are Number One .

Vicksburg **Post**, July 23

We're Lowest, By Far!

Jackson **Clarion-Ledger**, July 23

National Press Ignores
FBI Mississippi Report

Columbus **Commercial Dispatch**,
Aug. 4

Our Crime Record

State	Crimes Per 100,000 Pop. In 1962	Crimes Per. 100,000 Pop. In 1963
Mississsippi	446.4	393.2
North Dakota	410.4	472.9

Natchez Democrat, Nov. 15

WASHINGTON (UPI) — Mississippi's crime rate during 1963 was the nation's lowest, according to the Federal Bureau of Investigation's annual report issued Monday.

Paradoxically, the r e p o r t showed that Mississippians murder each other at a rate far exceeding many major cities around the nation.

There was an average of 7.2 murders per 100,000 Mississippi residents in 1963, compared to 3.8 in New York, 3.3 in Michigan, 5.1 in Illinois and 10.1 in Alabama.

Columbus **Commercial Dispatch**,
July 21

So — whether you are talking about murder, rape, assualt, robbery, t h i e f t, or anything else — anything that comes under the heading of crime — anything that adds up to lawlessness — the states from whence these invaders come have more of it by far than Mississippi.

Hattiesburg American, July 28

By Congressman Abernethy,

There has been a noticeable lack of interest on the part of the national press that the FBI Crime Report revealed Mississippians to be the most law-abiding people in the United States

Columbus **Commercial Dispatch**,
Sept. 4

Ted Polumbaum

Vandals Ruin Signs Along County's Highways

The Coahoma County Road department has been plagued by recent vandalism that has been responsible for the destruction or damaging of about 25 per cent of its road signs.

These two wrecks occurred in Beat 1 where a stop sign and a danger sign, both marked with reflector material, were torn down.

Other signs have been "shot to pieces," the road superintendent said.

Clarksdale Press Register,

Nov. 6

'SAFEST YEAR' IS PLANNED

West Point **Times Leader,**
Oct. 28

Tell 'em on Tags

Tom Douglas has come up with a good suggestion. He thinks the 1965 Mississippi tags (which are just a few months away) should read: "Nation's Lowest Crime Rate". He has sent a telegram to Governor Paul Johnson making this suggestion.

It's an excellent idea. We would like to see it adopted.

Vicksburg Post, July 23

Local man unloads on Life Magazine

F. E. Saucier, 417 Mabel St., provided The American with the following copy of a letter he mailed this week to the editor of Life Magazine.

Where in the world did you get your information about Mississippi?

Was it from Eugene Read of the National Association for the Advancement of Colored People? In a speech published nationwide Eugene described Mississippi as hell and said all the people of Mississippi did was ride around flashing guns. Well, Eugene is off base, to put it mildly.

We in Mississippi know that practically every Negro here has one or two guns bought with Communist money mostly, but it is hard for a white man in Mississippi to get a permit to carry a gun — I know because I have tried.

Hattiesburg American, July 23

* Nothing was done about the idea of using the phrase "nation's lowest crime rate" on license plates

Assistant Police Chief Roy Tootle said details in both incidents are incomplete, but the shots were reportedly fired from passing cars.

Hattiesburg American, Aug. 13

Unidentified witnesses said a young white man shot McGhee. They said the shot was fired from a station wagon carrying two white men.

Biloxi-Gulfport **Herald,** Aug. 23

MOSS POINT. Miss. (UPI) — A teen-age Negro girl was wounded last night when gunfire from a passing car greeted a crowd leaving a Negro voter registration meeting.

Jackson **Daily News,** July 7

MERIDIAN, Miss. (AP) — FBI and city investigators probed the firing of a shotgun into a house where two white civil rights workers slept early Monday.

Witnesses told investigators an old-model car halted briefly in front of the house and then drove off.

Laurel Leader-Call, Sept. 1

At Batesville, a tear-gas bomb thrown from a passing car hit the roof of a Negro dwelling and went off in the back yard.

Biloxi-Gulfport **Herald,** Sept. 5

NATCHEZ, Miss., Sept 25 — (UPI) — Police said an explosion ripped a hole in the lawn at the home of Mayor John J. Nosser tonight, followed by a similar blast at a Negro's home about a mile away.

"It was something thrown from a car," said Desk Sgt. Dennis Lewis. "But we don't know much about it yet."

Tupelo **Journal,** Sept. 27-28

Gun Safety-A Few Points

State Man Fatally Shot During Trial in Court

McComb **Enterprise-Journal,** Sept. 16

Constable Says He Shot Man Who Resisted Arrest

Laurel **Leader-Call,** Oct. 30

'Bloody Hitchhiker' Held In Shooting

Meridian **Star,** Nov. 24

Robert Fletcher

Curbs On Weapons Protect Citizens

Vicksburg **Post,** Oct. 23

* Then there were assorted crimes that had to be looked after, too, and many were shootings

Neshoba **Democrat,** Aug. 20

56

On What Should Not Be Done

Columbus **Commercial Dispatch,**
Nov. 1

ROLLING FORK — Funeral services for Mrs. Pauline E. Brown, 51, who was shot to death Thursday night in her home in Grace, Miss., when her small grandchild accidentally discharged a high-powered rifle, will be held at 2 p.m. today at the Assembly of God Church at Hampton, Miss.

Vicksburg Post, Nov. 28

Attacked with a walking stick, an 18-year old white grocery clerk shot a 50-year old Negro man to death here at about 8:45 a.m. Friday.

The youth told investigating officers Lindsey was well known at the store and had frequently caused trouble. He said Lindsey came to the store Thursday afternoon and demanded two $50 checks, which he said President Johnson and Barry Goldwater had sent to the store for him, Robinson said.

Laurel Leader-Call, Sept. 25

... He said he fired one shot with a 32-revolver and the knocking stopped.

Norman called the sheriff's office after he had opened the door and found the body of Coleman.

WEBB told Judge Smith he thought the case should be aired by the grand jury because "a knock on the door doesn't require a shot in the dark."

Delta Democrat Times, Nov. 6

JACKSON, Miss. (AP) — Two white men were charged with assault and battery with intent to kill Monday in the shooting of a Negro farm laborer April 5.

Fuller gained freedom under a $2,000 property bond signed by George and John Nosser, sons of Natchez Mayor John Nosser, the Hinds County sheriff's office records showed.

Greenwood Commonwealth,
Oct. 27

Asst. Dist. Atty. John Fox III told the jury in closing arguments that Hawkins and another white youth, Marcus Perkins, went into the Negro section of Jackson "for the pure simple purpose of shooting Negroes. I don't believe this is the sort of activity that should occur in this city."

**Pascagoula-Moss Point
Chronicle,** Nov. 18

JACKSON, Miss. (AP) — Dr. A. E. Holmes, well - known Terry physician, shot himself fatally Saturday night after a boast to play Russian roulette "if Ole Miss didn't win the football game."

Meridian Star, Oct. 25

VICKSBURG, Miss., Nov. 2 (UPI) —A local white man faced assault charges Monday in connection with the shooting of a 14-year-old Negro near the site of the Cairo salvage operation.

A witness, another Negro boy, and Marshall told officers that the shooting occurred when Marshall failed to say "sir" to Keen.

Tupelo Journal, Nov. 3

Officers said Stephen Greece and Martin McDonald were wounded while on a hayride over the weekend outside of Meridian.

Greece was hit in the leg and the same shot slammed into the abdomen of McDonald. It was not known where the shot came from.

Starkville News, Nov. 17

PONTOTOC — (Special) — A Pontotoc County youth is being held in the county jail in connection with the Saturday night fatal shooting of his 47-year old father: Norvel Salmon.

The Sheriff said the boy said he "was tired of hearing his father fussing."

Tupelo Journal, Oct. 19

Prisoners Hold Drunk Party At County Jail

Corinth **Corinthian**, Sept. 17

Booze Said Smuggled In Rear Window

Sources Claim Teen-age Girls Did A Striptease

Prisoners at the county jail staged a drunken party Wednesday night with paint thinner and whisky smuggled in through a rear window, it was reported this morning by a number of usually - reliable sources.

The sources said also that two teen-age girls, who have been held at the jail for several weeks for juvenile officers, performed a striptease for the benefit of male prisoners and later passed out nude in their cell.

Sherff S. C. Wilbanks denied that the incidents took place and said, "Absolutely no beer or whisky was consumed at the jail last night and nobody did a striptease."

Enemy Is Afraid Of Mississippi

MERIDIAN STAR:

Why has so much been said about MISSISSIPPI?

Many are interested in knowing why so much has been said about Mississippi. It is very obvious that attention has been given to Mississippi on purpose and out of proportion to equal and even greater problems elsewhere: In spite of the bad folk who live in Mississippi, we still have the lowest or second lowest crime rate in the nation. Furthermore we are the only dry state in our nation.

It is clear that because there are so many God fearing people in Mississippi, who are willing to humble themselves before God and fear NO MAN, the enemy is afraid of MISSISSIPPI. This is why they are crying to the top of their voices for help to break us. The enemy needs to know that the Bible teaches that five God-fearing people can chase 1000 workers for the Devil. Praise The Lord for Mississippi Christians who will stand true until death. Praise The Lord. WILLIE DENNIS, Pastor, First Southern Methodist, Philadelphia, Mississippi.

Meridian Star, July 24

However, one law officer and several elected officers whose duties keep them closely informed on situations at the jail said the party definitely took place.

The officer said he was at the jail last night and saw prisoners at cell windows. "They were certainly intoxicated," he said.

It was reported this morning that the prisoners made such a mess deputies spent nearly an hour cleaning up cells.

Youth Counselor Joe B. Mitchell said this morning he would investigate the part of the two girls in the alleged incident.

Corinth **Corinthian**, Sept. 17

Corinth **Corinthian**, Sept. 14

Legal Beer Is

Crackdown On Moonshine Nets 329 Stills, 87 Arrests

Jackson **Clarion-Ledger**, Dec. 1

'Moonshine' big killer in state

Moonshine Discovered By Cub Scouts

WALNUT GROVE, Miss. Three Cub Scouts on their way to a den meeting in Walnut Grove last week discovered 15 gallons of moonshine whisky.

Meridian Star, Nov. 11

New Tax Stamp For Bootleggers

JACKSON, Miss. (AP) — A new state regulation went into effect today for Mississippi bootleggers.

From now on, their illegal liquor must carry a state tax stamp or they are liable to get in trouble with the law.

The tax stamp was decreed by the Mississippi Tax Commission to enable its men to distinguish between legal illegal liquor and the strictly illegal type.

Biloxi-Gulfport **Herald**, Dec. 2

JACKSON, Miss. (AP) — A revenuer says medical autopsies would show a lot of "natural" deaths in Mississippi are really due to the low grade of moonshine booze in the state.

Jarvis L. Brewer, supervisor of the alcohol-tobacco tax division for the state, said laboratory tests on several hundred samples of moonshine found more than 25. per cent of it is slow poison.

Hattiesburg American, Dec. 2

An intersting footnote to Mississippi's ridiculous liquor law was brought to light over the weekend.

Records show that one of every five persons admitted to state mental institutions is an alcoholic.

As William Peart, Jackson Daily News reporter, once wrote; "Mississippi is as dry as a martini."

And we have the alcoholics to prove it.

McComb **Enterprise-Journal,** Dec. 1

Stop Sweeping The Dirt Under the Rug

MERIDIAN STAR:

The black market tax on illegal liquor, the 230 beer licenses sold for illegal gambling in Mississippi is a disgrace. Small wonder Mississippi gets the kind of publicity it does from all the news medias. We have about the highest state sales tax, about the lowest paid teachers, about the highest automobile registration fee, about the lowest unemployment benefits, about the highest gasoline tax and the lowest per capita income of the 50 states.

For one thing, we are not smarter than the other 49 states; let s face it. All the other 49 states collect revenue from alcoholic beverages in a legal and above the board manner and apply the money where it helps all their citizens;

Let's stop sweeping the dirt under the rug and thinking like an ostrich when it puts its head in the sand thinking it's hid. Just look what it leaves showing. E. G. D., Meridian.

Meridian Star, Oct. 25

*And the bootleggers required some time. Twenty per cent of those admitted to Mississippi's mental institutions are alcoholic . . . in the Union's only dry state

Defeated 1,281 To 771

Corinth **Corinthian**, Sept. 16

Rising Right Now

'Miss Vicksburg' Named 'Miss Mississippi' 1964

Clarksdale **Press Register**, July 27

VICKSBURG, Miss (UPI) — The new Miss Mississippi says she will tell the world her state is not "going to rise again but is rising right now."

Dark-haired, talented Judith Simono of Vicksburg declared here Saturday night she would urge persons outside the state not to criticize Mississippians until they visit the state.

"I would urge them not to criticize for what they read but to come home with me to see Mississippi for themselves," said the brown-eyed beauty, who apparently scored high on answers to questions asked the semifinalists to test their intellect.

Columbus **Commercial Dispatch**, July 27

Wide World Photos

✱ Football and assorted queens are a zestful part of Mississippi life

Miss Rosanne Burleson State Welcome Symbol

Meridian Star, Aug. 2

Football Season, 1964 Style Opens In Starkville Tonight

Starkville News, Sept. 4

Ole Miss Football Pep Rally Turns Into Riot

OXFORD, Miss. (AP) — Students fired up by a football pep rally kept the Unversity of Mississippi campus in violent turmoil for hours early today.

The uproar was a sort of combination panty raid, police stoning and "car rolling."

The car belonged to Burns Tatum, chief of campus police. It was overturned and barrel-rolled down a hill. He wasn't in it at the time.

The raid, good humored at first, turned angry as the night wore on. Bricks and bottles were thrown at police. One officer was gashed on the head by a brick.

Ole Miss has two Negro students who room together in one of the men's dormitories. Smith said they were not involved in the turmoil in any way.

"What this was," he said, "was football."

McComb Enterprise-Journal, Oct. 3

Dear Editor:

Public education in Mississippi has been captured by coaches!

The capture of our schools by coaches has led to the most corrupt and closed political organization in our state. Any man who enters the teaching field, unless a coach, is subjected to all kinds of prejudices and unfair treatment. Its's hard to teach honesty when you have to drive 100 miles a day because no housing is available except for coaches who make twice as much as you do and teach half as much.

Applications of good teachers are ignored while the jobs are held open for a coach regardless of his teaching qualifications.

All of this has resulted in the railroading of school appropriations into vastly over-emphasized athletic programs, that in the end, do little more than line the pockets of these coaches.

It can be stopped: provided we, the people, admit the deplorable condition of our schools: provided we realize that a coach is no tin-god, and pay him to coach while we also pay teachers to teach.

We have a choice, how many of us have the guts to make it?

J. D. C.
Coldwater, Miss.
B.S. 'Miss. State'.

Jackson Clarion-Ledger, Aug. 8

RESOLUTION

WHEREAS THE GULFPORT HIGH SCHOOL FOOTBALL TEAM, THE COMMODORES, have won the South Big Eight Conference Football championship for 1964 and will play for the Big Eight Championship on November 27, 1964, and

WHEREAS, the Gulfport City Council desires to show that it, as well as all the people of the City, are proud of the accomplishments, the sportsmanship, and the ability shown by the GULFPORT COMMODORES, and

WHEREAS, the City of Gulfport is extremely proud of Head Coach Lindy Callahan, Coach Leo Jones, Coach Bert Jenkins, and Coach Ray Bishop, and of the fine representation that these coaches and the Commodores have given the City of Gulfport on the athletic fields, and

WHEREAS, it is our sincere desire to show our appreciation to and pride in these fine young athletes and their coaches, and to wish them well for their future endeavors,

NOW THEREFORE, be it resolved by the Gulfport City Council, duly assembled in official session, that we extend to the GULFPORT HIGH SCHOOL COMMODORES our congratulations on their fine accomplishments, and assure them of the support, admiration, and pride that we of the City of Gulfport have for them and their coaches.

BE IT further resolved that a copy of this Resolution be forwarded to Head Coach Lindy Callahan and to the local press.

UNANIMOUSLY adopted this the 17th day of November, 1964.

R. B. Meadows Jr.
MAYOR

H. E. Blakeslee
COMMISSIONER

J. H. McManus
COMMISSIONER

Biloxi-Gulfport Herald, Nov. 23

Steve Schapiro

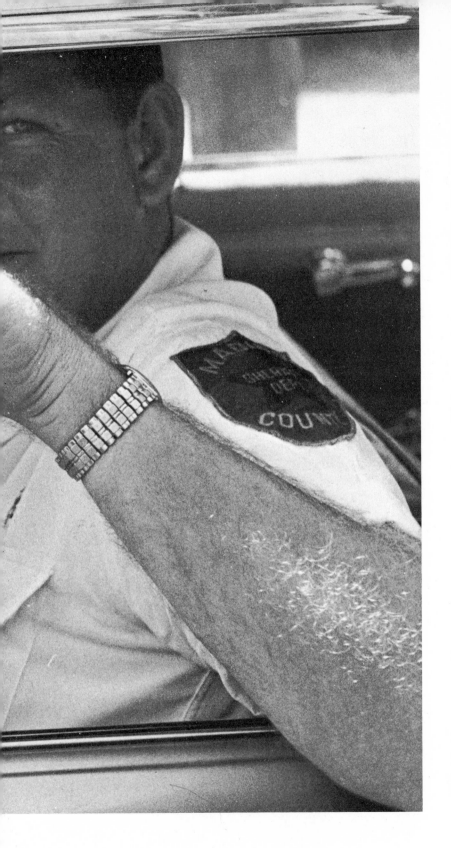

✱ There is concern about military occupation

Dear Editor:

All summer long you and your columnists have been screaming about the COFO workers and their plans to remake Mississippi. I had been paying no attention to you, considering this some more of your usual shrill nonsense.

But then I read in the August, 22, 1964 issue of THE NEW REPUBLIC, a liberal Democratic magazine that has a privileged ear to all the civil-rights activities, an article by Christopher Jencks, in which was stated:

"Every activity of the Summer - Project-voter registration- the freedom schools, the community centers, the study of federal programs in the state, the effort to proselytize among poor whites — all relate to the overriding aim of redistributing political power . . . The new 'liberal' Democratic party could and federal spending . . . to make use its control of federal offices changes in the state."

They want to "give Mississippi Negroes a major voice in their own destinies before they despair, making them part of 'power structure.' Only the federal government has the power to do this; certainly white Mississippians will not do it voluntarily . . ." What would make the federal government move in time? Only killing, I fear . . . It will probably take repeated and dramatic white violence against Negroes to elicit the necessary federal action . . ."

Did you hear all that, Mr. Editor? All you columnists and reporters got that? And all you folks out in reader-land, you CCs and KKKs, you rednecks and nigger-haters and mob-instigators, you night-riders and knocking cops and slobs — you get that too!

COFO and the Federal Government want to put this state under military occupation, and then they'll make you dance to whatever tune they call. They are looking for the excuse to do it. Don't give them the excuse.

Jno. Q. Public
Jackson

Jackson **Clarion-Ledger**, Sept. 10

State in Need of 'New Money'

McComb **Enterprise-Journal**, Dec. 2

State Had To Borrow $5 Million

Biloxi-Gulfport **Herald**, Sept. 2

State In Debt $202,098,000

Laurel **Leader-Call**, Oct. 13

State Has $28 Million Less Than 4 Years Ago

Tupelo **Journal**, July 15

Tunica County Is Reported To Be Poorest In Nation

Greenwood **Commonwealth**, Nov. 24

Then there is the problem of mental retardation. It is known from preliminary studies that there are 60,000 mentally retarded persons in the state.

At present the state's only institution for the mentally retarded is Ellisville State School. It can house 1,200 patients. Another 900 patients — all Negro — are being cared for in a building at Whitfield.

McComb **Enterprise-Journal**, Nov. 30

JACKSON (UPI)— Mississippi today has the highest number of cases of tuberculosis within a decade, it was announced today by the State Board of Health.

Grenada **Sentinel-Star**, Dec. 10

This state is first in the number of man-caused fires. Mississippi has held that position for many years, according to Lee.

Delta Democrat-Times, Dec. 7

JACKSON (UPI) — State Welfare Commissioner Evelyn Gandy said Saturday that welfare payments for June totaled $4,521,315, a decrease of $982 from May.

Miss Gandy said an average grant of $37.23 was made to the aged and $43.97 to the blind; and 66,033 dependent children received an average of $13.30.

Pascagoula-Moss Point **Chronicle**, July 6

The state has got to stay in the black, said the governor. To help assure this, he said, he appointed a marketing council last week which will encourage the establishment of plants to process state resources wherever possible and to seek new markets for state products in Central and South America.

Hattiesburg American, Aug. 11

A comparison with the balance today, less the $6 million, showed the state spent almost $4 million more than it took in during the past 12 months.

Jackson **Clarion-Ledger**, July 2

State Has Highest Infant Mortality Rate In Nation

Natchez Democrat, Nov. 28

What '75 x 75' Means

An announced goal at the PEP (Programming Economic Progress) meeting over the state is expressed as "75 x 75" — which interpreted means that Mississippi's per capita income should be 75 percent of the national per capita income by 1975.

Corinth **Corinthian**, Dec. 15

"In 1962, Mississippi's per capita income of $1,262 ($1,285 in current dollars) was 2.5 times the 1929 figure, and was 54.3 percent of the national average per capita of $2,324 ($2,366 in current dollars)."

Biloxi-Gulfport **Herald**, Aug. 15

Mississippi ranks 49th among states in banking resources per capita.

Biloxi-Gulfport **Herald**, Nov. 7

Special Session Forecast

"I THINK that we may be called to untangle the state highway problem," Sen. Caraway said. "It appears that the highway department has too many miles of highway to look after and not enough money," he explained.

"Of course," Rep. Merideth said, "the session might be called to investigate the state's financial position. As you know we are having to borrow money right now."

Delta Democrat-Times, Dec. 11

Tom Wakayama, SNCC

*... **Mississippi is troubled by many problems**

Mr. John D. Smith
Highway Commissioner,
Southern District
State of Mississippi
Dear Sir:

You don't know me because I live on State Highway No. 600 between Ceasar and Necaise and I know you haven't been on this particular section of State Highway within your district or you would have done something to it, because if there ever was a State Highway that everyone should be ashamed of, this is it.

I have your campaign promise before me in which you stated that this road between Ceasar and Necaise would be fixed during your next term of office, if elected. A year has passed and still no survey or anything

Now I know everybody wants a road and I also know funds are limited, but assuming you are a man of honor and not a small petty politician, I believe if you would take time out from your busy schedule and take a ride over this Highway, I know you would do something for us, if it's only to put some gravel on it, pull the ditches where it will drain and do something to these bridges before somebody gets killed, perhaps a busload of school children.

Yours truly,
J.F.McE.
Picayune, Mississippi

P. S. Don't come in your own car, borrow an old one or if possible come in a jeep or swamp buggy.

Jackson **Clarion-Ledger**, Aug. 14

$669,887 Grant   To Assist School Dropouts In Five Area Counties

Tupelo **Journal**, Nov. 25

Mississippi Feed Grain Farmers Get Six Million

Laurel Leader-Call, Sept. 2

Bribing The States

There are some things not for sale. Mississippians are not going to bow and scrape and kiss a lot of Washington boots in exchange for a portion of that which is already ours. Principles and votes are not yet for sale in Mississippi. And we hope they never will be!

West Point **Times Leader**, Nov. 11

Mississippi paid only $307,962,000 into the U.S. Treas. last year, got back from Washington $1,160,920,000 in the fiscal year 1964. This included $126,000,000 in military contracts; $94,100,000 for space projects; $11,959,000 for civilian supply contracts; $148,546,000 to pay the salaries of federal employees in Mississippi; $10,160,000 in food for the needy; $7,344,414 for school luncheons; $10,714,000 for accelerated public works to take care of employment, and about $23,000,000 for educational construction, college loans, and vocational training.

McComb **Enterprise-Journal**, Nov. 12

Norris McNamara

Mississippi Prepares For Major Role In The U.S. Space Program

Jackson **Clarion-Ledger**, Oct. 9

✳ Mississippi is "dead set against the Federal Government," but she benefited from $1,660,920,000 from Washington in 1964

Mississippians Dead Set Against LBJ On All Issues, Even Tax Cut

Tupelo **Journal,** Nov. 25

Dear Editor:

We must not deceive ourselves (nor permit the Bolshevik Revolutionaries to deceive us) thats imply because the National Tyrant is far away in Washington, wearing a white shirt and neat tie, with a servile and sympathetic National Press to build a false image of holiness around him, that he is less dangerous than our local tyrant down at the courthouse with his chew of tobacco and unpressed kahkis, for in truth, that National Tyrant is ten thousand times as dangerous, and his pious mouthings are but a mask for his dedicated efforts to increase his Power and decrease our Liberty.

Yours truly,
R. J. T.
Jackson, Miss.

Jackson **Clarion-Ledger,** Oct. 15

Dear Editor:

I note in Drew Pearson's column of yesterday the snide suggestion that Mississippi should be boycotted economically— Why the simple-minded SOB —doesn't he realize that the greatest Negro population (practically 50-50 with the whites) is in this state and doesn't he realize that when the "white boss" goes broke, the colored man goes broke with him, it has always been thus (and then what is to come of that "vast program of improvement" for the negro race???)

Do you think for a minute that these big Northern Banks and millionaire investors, are going to let "Washington" hurt their investments??? And the best thing the U.S. could do with such as Pearson (and his ilk) is to send them to Russia, wherein their hearts really are imbedded.

J. R. (Col.) Cofield
(The Ole Miss "photog"
Colonel).

Jackson Clarion-Ledger, Nov. 14

You people may find his article of interest, as follows:

"Mississippians, as in the past, will always be courteous to travelers passing through our State, and such courteous treatment was accorded Ladybird Johnson on the Gulf Coast last week.

One of the most sickening of her statements on the whistle stop campaign was, "When I see some kid with a Goldwater banner", she said cunningly, "I swap him Johnson candy for it." That is typical of the Johnson's principles a free handout for a vote. That is the Communists way, and the Socialists way. Something for nothing!

Jackson **Clarion-Ledger,** Oct. 21

Dear Mr. Hederman:

If you and your paper would use a little more energy in educating the people of Mississippi to getting in step with the wonderful basic principles of the good old U.S.A., you would do your state and country a great service.

Mississippi could be a truly great state — and you could help the backward people of inner Mississippi, in particular, in responding to equality of all under the law.

There must be something you can find good about the U. S., Washington, the Democrats, the Supreme Court, NAACP, CORE, Union bosses, big business, etc.

A newcomer to this great state,

J. R.
No. 411, Biloxi.

Jackson Clarion-Ledger, Nov. 19

Dear Editor:

It would have been appropriate for all flags to fly at half mast on November 4 in observance of the death of freedom in our land.

But console youselves, my fellow Mississippian. By rejecting the man who promised to put the interest of America and Americans first and choosing as president the appeasing internationalist who is motivated by expediency, we won the gratitude of our vaccillating, sponging allies and our scornful enemies who voiced relief at our "sensibleness."

So stifle your patriotism. It is no longer considered a desirable trait, but rather one of selfishness. We are not Mississippians or even Americans. We are citizens of the Community of the Brotherhood of the World. Does that sweeten the bitter taste in your mouths?

Mrs. B. L.

Lena, Miss.

Jackson **Clarion-Ledger,** Nov. 13

Some residents of North Jackson found a green, mimeographed circular on their doorsteps Saturday calling on them to "wake up."

The unsigned, one-page circular charged "tyranny, Treachery, Trickery, treason is the order of the day in Washington: Honor, integrity, race, country and America's Christian religion are becoming outmoded."

". . . have you wondered how pauper Lyndon became a multimillionaire in less than 30 years though he has never been anything but a salaried government employe?"

Jackson **Clarion-Ledger,** July 5

67

Your hatred hurts you.

For every action there is a reaction. If we love we are loved. If we give we are given. When we learn this and believe it we have learned God's plan for us.

No man can live alone. He needs his neighbor. God told us this many times, "Love thy neighbor as thyself." God also told us who our neighbor was . . . everyone, even our enemy.

It is hard for us to accept this unless we realize that our hatred hurts us. Hatred drives out love. That is why God told us to love one another. The more we love the closer we come to God who is perfect love. Truly we are our brother's keeper.

Dear Editor:
If Jesus came to earth as a Negro, I believe he would live as a good segregationist. We have many Negroes doing that now.

The Negro forgets that when he gives the white man a dollar in the cafes, hotels, motels, and stores that he is hurting a Negro business man.

Christ as a Negro would not go hungry, cold, thirsty, uneducated or friendless. Negro business men could take care of him.

Integration would lead to the cause of the failure of many Negro business men. Only thru segregation can we have equality.
Sincerely,
The White Race
Columbia, Miss.

Jackson **Clarion-Ledger**, Aug. 18

Advertisement, Biloxi-Gulfport
Herald, Oct. 24

'Let Integration Alone,' Says Quitmanite

Meridian Star, Sept. 3

Dear Editor:

Years ago, as a Jew, Jesus Christ walked the hillsides of Israel where he was despised, rejected, and eventually crucified. If he came to Mississippi in 1964, as a Negro, how would we professing Christians receive him?

Then spake Jesus unto them and said, "I was hungry and ye refused me admittance to your restaurants; I was thirsty and ye would not serve me; I was of the minority and ye offered me no friendship; I craved learning and ye would not let me enter your schools; I was tired but no hotel would receive me; I was your neighbor and ye loved me not; I was a citizen deserving equal rights but ye kept them from me; I paid taxes and went into the service of this country but the benefits thereof ye gave me not; Ye proclaimed that ye worshipped my Father, yet I could not worship with thee."

Then they answered him saying, "Lord, when did we these things unto you?"

And Jesus answered them; "Inasmuch as ye have done it unto the least of these, my brethren, ye have done it unto me."

Ghandi once said, "I love your Christ, but I hate your Christianity."

Need I say more?

Yours truly,
T. S.
Clinton

Jackson **Clarion-Ledger**, Aug. 11

Dear Editor:

This has reference to the letter of T. S. of Clinton.

Our Lord said nothing about restaurants. There are excellent restaurants all over Mississippi operated by Negroes serving Negroes. Maybe Theresa doesn't believe that Negroes can cook!

Our Lord said nothing about being in a minority. In fact, as a Jew, he was in a majority in Palestine and he criticized the woman having an "issue of blood" because though non-Jewish she seemed to expect the same benefits as were reserved for the Jewish people.

Our Lord said nothing about schools. Mississippi has excellent schools staffed by competent Negro teachers to teach Negro children. Theresa must feel that Negroes are not qualified to teach.

Our Lord said nothing about being denied the right to worship in the Temple . . . he wasn't . . . but non-Jews were denied this right. Theresa must feel that the capable Negro clergy of Mississippi are not capable of expounding the Gospel.

I will give $5 to any Negro organization that Theresa names if she will cite the chapter and verse in either the King James or the Duoay version where the words she quotes are found as she quotes them in her letter.

Need I say more?

E. L. W.   Pine St.
Jackson, Mississippi

Jackson **Clarion-Ledger**, Aug. 15

✳ Quoting from the Bible is Mississippi pastime

MERIDIAN STAR:

Our Negroes are being misled. It was an abomination for an Egyptian to eat with a Hebrew. Gen. 43:32. Joseph and the Egyptian ate separately. So if we whites and Negroes want to be blessed of God, we better let integration alone. — MRS. C. C. R„ Quitman.

Meridian Star, Sept. 3

God Is The Creator Of Color Contrast

MERIDIAN STAR:

Regarding the "Heart Not Color—Important" letter of July 17th in the Meridian Star, first, and most important—God is the creator of color contrast.

I wish to quote a passage from the July 17th letter, "If all were of the same color, the effect would be monotonous and depressing". Now, isn't that exactly what the integrationists want—for everyone to be the same?

God, in his infinite wisdom, saw fit to segregate the races—and now, man, through his limited reasoning and Darwin theories tries to explain away God's rules of nature and man. Sincerely, MRS. W. W., Collinsville, Miss.

Meridian Star, Aug. 30

Dear Editor:

...Mixing of races does not come from the Bible, but from the Communists, N. A. A. C. P. and others who have been misinformed. There are misled people who actually believe that the Bible says "God made all men equal." This is not true. It is not in the Bible.

Again, they say that "God is no respecter of persons." That refers to salvation and not to equality of people!

Let us relieve ourselves of the Christian Life Commission and go on with our task of evangelizing the world.

A. A. Kitchings, Ph.D.
Formerly, Head of Foreign Languages in Mississippi College, Presently, Pastor Spring Hill Baptist Church

Jackson **Clarion-Ledger**, July 16

Spiritual Emphasis Week

West Point **Times Leader**, Dec. 2

Police Planning
Big Gospel Sing

Natchez Democrat, Sept. 27

All-Night Gospel Sing Slated Here

Jackson **Clarion-Ledger**, Nov. 5

Trying To Get To Heaven In Wrong Way?

The Old Testament prophets completely reverse the idea that a person who relies on prayers, on meetings, on material gifts, and on solemn church services is good enough.

Isn't it strange that the Prophets and Jesus both place so little emphasis on theological ideas, on sacred institutions, and cherished beliefs?

Isn't it strange that rather than encouraging the type of goodness and the type of church activities in which we tend to engage that the great prophets and Jesus talk about widows and orphans and ask, "who is your neighbor?"

The chief characteristic of prophetic thought is that God is involved in history and that He is concerned with man. If we want to be "good" in the Biblical sense of that term we must be involved in the problems of the world and we must be deeply concerned with the people of the world.

Our God is not a spectator. He is a participant in the world. If we are to be like Him we must show mercy to others and seek justice for individual men and women.

Tupelo **Journal**, Sept. 21

All Night Prayer Set Wednesday

At 8:30 p.m. various members of the church will come for half hour periods to pray. This prayer chain will continue all night.

The items to be prayed for are:

1. God sent, Christ centered, Holy spirit impowered revival.
2. Recognition of God in our national life.
3. Allegiance to Constitutional Government.
4. Leaders who are faithful to God, Jesus Christ, Country, and who study God's Word.
5. Leaders with wisdom to discern good from evil; the courage to resist the evil and do the good.
6. That God's will be done in the November 3 election.

Vicksburg Post, Oct. 27

Adult Thrust Session Set By Baptists

Jackson **Clarion-Ledger**, Sept. 12

Ladies night tonight at revival

Hattiesburg American, Oct. 7

Pack-A-Pew For Revival

West Point **Times Leader**, July 15

✲ **Mississippi goes to church**

Cross Burning At Ruleville Brings Up Some Questions

Jackson **Clarion-Ledger,**
Aug. 23

Rev. Lynch Tells of U.S. Problem

More people are attending church today than ever before but that is not the most important thing, says the Rev. Bob Lynch, pastor of Central Baptist Church.

The question is "what are we doing during the week," he told the McComb Rotary Club at its noon meeting Wednesday.

On the subject of civil rights, the Rev. Mr. Lynch said the love referred to in the Bible does not relate to integration. Criticizing ministers who come south to advocate civil rights, the Rev. Mr. Lynch said "I don't have time to go somewhere else and tell them how to do. I stay busy at home."

McComb **Enterprise-Journal,**
July 9

If A Man Prays Right,

Advertisement, West Point
Times Leader, July 17

Business Of God Dwarfs All Others

Tupelo **Journal,** Nov. 17-18

It's refreshing to note that the churches of Mississippi are displaying a growth pattern that reflects both dedication and determination.

All over Mississippi, you see new Churches, of all denominations, under construction. It's a wonderful indication. There's nothing wrong with this nation that a good moral and spiritual reawakening can't cure! **Starkville News,** Sept. 9

Advertisement,
Laurel Leader-Call, Aug. 29

John Else, a member of the coordinating committee on morals and civil rights of the International Convention of Christian Churches (Disciples of Christ), testified that churches in the Moss Point-Pascagoula area are no longer used for NAACP or civil rights meetings because they were threatened with cancellation of insurance.

Laurel Leader-Call, Oct. 22

NAACP members were halted and refused entrance to the First Baptist Church, Jackson.

The solution

Neither lawless acts from within nor the efforts of well-meaning groups and individuals from the outside will ever solve Mississippi's racial problems. Rather the solution lies with Christian people of both races in Mississippi "acting in the spirit of Christ, and under the principles of God."

Hattiesburg American, Oct. 8

Can He Live Wrong?

Advertisement, West Point
Times Leader, July 17

A Mississippi State University survey showed that the state's churches average one for every 289 persons. The natonal average is one for every 814 persons.

Pascagoula-Moss Point
Chronicle, Nov. 11

* **Mississippi churches had problems right on their own doorsteps**

73

Outsiders Frowned On By Mississippi Baptists

Meridian Star, Nov. 11

Baptists Hit Out At Racial Extremists

Starkville News, Nov. 12

Dear Editor:

The vermiform appendix gets its name from the shape of a worm and has no known useful function. Its surgical removal is called an appendectomy.

Southern Baptists have a vermiform appendix which, according to the opinion of many Southern Baptists, needs an appendectomy.

Why the Christian Life Commission ever came into being, is the puzzle for many Southern Baptists.

This Commission never fails to inject the race issue into our deliberations, as a convention. Such issue is divisive and absolutely unnecessary in our convention. It has no place in our discussions. We need unity and coherence, not strife and factionalism.

So long as we have this unnecessary vermiform appendix, we shall have to resist recommendations which are unscriptural, unreasonable, and un-Baptistic.

Jackson Clarion-Ledger, July 16

MERIDIAN STAR:

please print the following in your paper as I am sure my denominational paper will not.

HOW LONG — HOW LONG? How long will we Southern Baptists continue to accept the views of our Southern Baptist Board and continue to use material recommended for study courses by them?

I must say the book, "ANOTHER COUNTRY" by James Baldwin is so filthy it should not be published, much less recommended by our Southern Baptist Board writers, as resource material for our young people. If you are reading this and have any doubt, come by and I will let you read for yourself. This offer is for MEN ONLY as I have too much respect for our women and youth to show them such VULGAR writing.

H. P.
Meridian, Miss.

Meridian Star, Aug. 10

To The Editor:

I read where the National Council of Churches is wanting to have the so called civil rights issue in the presidential campaign. They are not satisfied with sending their agitators to Mississippi. Now they want to make trouble on a larger scale. God help the American people when a group like this can operate under the name Church. Christian people had better wake up. I read my children's Sunday School lessons. They can wangle their way into them if we don't watch. We need to pray more and know what is being taught, not only in Church, but also in school.

Yours truly,
Mrs. M. R. K.
Laurel, Miss.

Laurel Leader-Call, Sept. 26

Prominent Baptist Delta Pastor Resigns

BELZONI (AP) — After 21 years as pastor, Chester A. Molpus has resigned from Belzoni's first Baptist Church, evidently because of a difference of opinion with the church membership over racial attitudes.

Molpus said, "I have arrived at the place where I, for my part, will not deny to a Negro who desires it the privilege of worshipping in the same church building with me. I cannot, for the life of me, imagine Jesus standing on the Church steps and turning a man away because of the color of his skin."

Jackson Clarion-Ledger, Oct. 29

White Chaplain Accepted Into Negro Group

JACKSON, Miss. (AP) — A controversial white chaplain at predominately Negro Tougaloo College has been accepted on trial into the Negro conference of the Methodist Church in Mississippi, officials said Thursday.

Biloxi-Gulfport Herald, July 7

Dr. W. Douglas Hudgins, pastor of the host church, told the convention the Baptist denomination needs a new effort in evangelism. He said the Baptists' rate of growth has dropped from a 29 per cent increase in 1949 to "a bare two per cent in 1963."

✳ The National Council of Churches staffed people at Oxford, Ohio, where civil rights workers trained, and later at Jackson, Miss., in conjunction with the "Mississippi Project"

Civil Rights Meet Is 'Bombed'

Delta Democrat-Times, Oct. 23

Explosive Drops On Rights Meet

Pascagoula-Moss Point Chronicle, Oct. 23

INDIANOLA, Miss. (UPI) A small airplane swooped over a building where 250 persons were attending a civil rights meeting last night and dropped an explosive that jarred the structure, a civil rights group claims.

An officer at the Indianola Police Department said he could give no information on the reported incident. "I don't know anything about it," he said. "I wasn't on duty when it happened."

Later, another police spokesman said the noise heard by the bi-racial group was caused by a "firecracker dropped from the plane."

Meridian Star, Oct. 23

Police Chief Brice Alexander was attending a special area meeting called by the Greenville Chamber of Commerce in Greenville at the time of the incident.

"This is not the first time an airplane has dropped flares or firecrackers," Chief Alexander reported. "We have had them drop them all over Indianola."

Delta Democrat-Times, Oct. 23

✳ **COFO workers set up community centers, freedom schools, and held voter registration rallies for Negroes**

Tom Wakayama, SNCC

COFO Hattiesburg meeting

Freedom House, Moss Point

Combat Group Waiting For Trouble At Natchez

Pascagoula-Moss Point **Chronicle**, July 1

THERE is an ominous air when you stand outside a civil rights rally, listen to the chant of "freedom now, freedom now," then talk to a grizzled white farmer five miles down the road who says, "I'll be damned if they get it."

Delta Democrat-Times, July 28

✱ Civil rights workers were warned not to move into the Natchez area. "Natchez is ready and waiting," one Natchezian said. "They've got enough scrap iron to sink a dozen bodies in the Mississippi until long after this long hot summer is over"

MERIDIAN STAR:
. . . Now, ask yourself another question, what is the meaning of the freedom they promise you? Does it merely mean the right to sit at a lunch counter with White people? Would you be happy with that? Would you want White people coming into your home to visit? How would you feel if they did? Would you feel cramped, ill at ease, or would it seem natural to you? Now what have you gained? You have freedom now, you're not in bondage, and I believe you'd rather go to Church and places of entertainment with people of your own race than to the same places with White people.

Those of you who already see through this know that God did not intend the races to mix or he would not have made us different.

Name withheld
Meridian Star, July 2

77

FREEDOM LIBRARY

HOURS - MON-FRI·3-5,7-8 p.m.
SAT·10-12 a.m.

One Man

Ted Polumbaum

Steve Schapiro

✳ Older persons as well as young teachers were used in freedom schools

Clifford Vaughs, SNCC

Herbert Randall

Deplores Disgraceful Treatment Of State

MERIDIAN STAR: Open letter to Gov. Paul Johnson:

The harassments of y o u r citizens by an invading army of left - wing degenerates and misguided college students who are not dry behind their political ears, is a national disgrace; and every decent American should rise up in wrath against it. Internal colonialism in our great nation in the 2t0h century is no longer tolerable.

As 6ne Californian. I offer my humble apologies and urge you, as governor of Mississippi, to round up the California contingent of com-rats and beatniks and the misguided youth, put them on a bus, and point it in the direction of California. Or better still, put them on a ship at Gulfport and head the ship toward Moscow. Sincerely. RALPH W. MC-INNIS. C h a i r m a n. California Committee to Combat Regional Bigotry, Outrigger Apartments. 1020 Delores St.. Apt. 38. Livermore, California.

Meridian Star, July 9

Dear Editor:

How any person could be a traitor to the white race by being a freedom worker is beyond me. How can a ·man or woman be traitor enough to his own race to support the cjvll rights bill is beyond me. When a white man or womari turns against his 6wn race, he is a traitor to that race. The white freedom workers have turned against the white race.

The people who passed the civil rights bill were for the most part white men. Were they true to their race? I don't believe so. Are the white men who try to enforce the civil rights bill true to the white race? I don't think so. We will have to start considering any congressman and senator who votes for sueh bills as traitors to the white race. Also for people who try to enforce the bill as traitors to us also.

In some counties in the South no white woman will be safe if the white traitors have their way. No white girl will be safe on any street in any town if the white traitors have their way.

Let's start voting anybody out of office unless he is for the white man first, last and always.
J. W. B.
Jackson, Miss.
Jackson Clarion-Ledger,
Sept. 23

Matt Herron

Steve Schapiro

'Freedom Schools' springing up throughout Mississippi

Hattiesburg American, July 10

JACKSON, Miss. (AP)—They call them schools, but there aren't any report cards, bells or football teams.

The students are Negroes. The teachers are white.

They are called "Freedom Schools"—part of the sweeping civil rights movement in Mississippi being directed by the Council of Federated Organiza-tions, which coordinates activities of the major civil rights groups.

One of the aims of the Freedom Schools is to help Negroes pass voter registration tests.

The teachers work from 8 a.m. until noon and again from 7:30 p.m. to 9:30 p.m. in night classes. Their classrooms are in Negro churches, garages and sometimes in private homes.

The schools are striving to teach subjects and ideas which a COFO spokesman says "are not normally available" to the Negro.

The students in the 8-12 age group study reading, writing, spelling, Negro history and general mathematics.

Those older can choose courses from the language arts, American history, social studies science and math.

Hattiesburg American, July 10

* Freedom schools offered instruction in remedial academic programs, contemporary issues and citizenship training, as well as practical subjects — typing, sewing, carpentry. For the very young there were games and story-telling

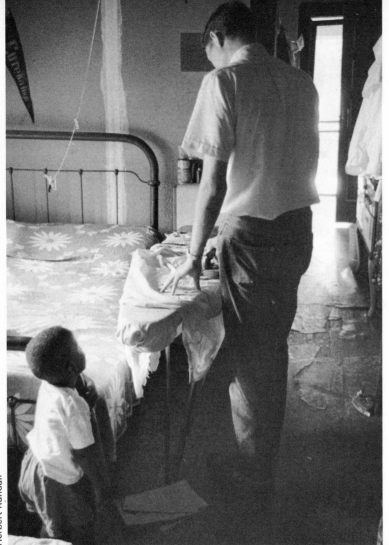

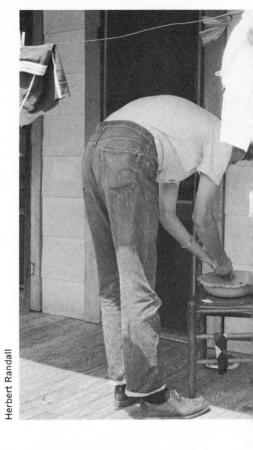

Matt Herron

✱ COFO workers cooked, washed
and ironed their own clothes
and lived the life of the Negro family

Herbert Randall

Herbert Randall

Arson In The House Of God

APPARENTLY most of our ministers have not felt compelled to speak as these houses of God were burned down, although their silence is perhaps only consistent with their usual approach to the trampling of Christ's doctrines by Mississippi's haters.

Let a church pledge be dropped or whiskey touched, and then hear the thunder roll from the pulpits. But let a place of God be desecrated by modern Huns and we hear not even a mild admonition.

As for the county lawmen in counties hardest hit by the arsonists, their usual response is that the conflagrations "have nothing to do with the race situation." This is said as though church burnings during the period of midnight to sun-up were commonplace in Mississippi prior to this summer.

Delta Democrat-Times, Aug. 2

Pressing his request for a temporary restraining order, Kunstler declared, "They burned another church in Pike County last night. That makes 10." (A Negro church was burned Tuesday night outside McComb in Pike County.)

"Those things are occurring all over the United States, for that matter," Judge Mize answered.

William Kuntzler, Attorney for COFO; U.S. District Judge Sidney Mize, **Meridian Star,** Aug. 23

✳ **Negro churches were used for voter registration rallies**

Bodies, Church Fires Keep Authorities Busy

Columbus **Commercial**
Dispatch, July 14

Coroner's Work Has Been Slow

Fred Diamond, Jackson County Coroner, reported this morning that June 11 was the date of the last death he investigated. He commented that this is the longest period of time since he took office that a death hasn't been reported under his jurisdiction.

Pascagoula-Moss Point
Chronicle, July 3

The workers had left Meridian that morning to investigate the burning of a Negro church near state Highway 16 near Philadelphia. They disappeared that night.

Delta Democrat-Times, Aug. 5

Mississippi, one of the most peaceful and law-abiding states in the United States, is being maligned in a manner without a parallel in the history of our country.

So far there is not a shred of evidence that a Mississippian laid a hand on either one of the three missing civil rights workers who went to Philadelphia to meddle in local affairs.

It is as clear as the noonday sun that the integrationists, the vote hunting politicians, the Communists and others are determined to punish Mississippi for its policies and way of life.

Jackson **Clarion-Ledger**, Aug. 30

Steve Schapiro

Mt. Zion Church in Philadelphia, visited by Michael Schwerner, Andrew Goodman and James Chaney on the day they disappeared

FLAMES DESTROY CHURCH IN DELTA

Laurel Leader Call, July 11

Klan Offers a Reward in Church Fire Cases

McComb Enterprise Journal,
July 27

J. E. Thornhill, wealthy Mississippi oil man who is considered in the McComb area to be the top Klan representative in this state, reports that he pulled out of the Klan three weeks ago because it apparently had lost control of its hoodlum rebels.

He "got out of the deal" on June 25, he said, because he objected to such activities as church burnings and house bombings as "not in the true spirit of the Ku Klux Klan."

Tupelo Journal, July 20

* Negro churches were burned and bombed in retaliation against voter registration

Church Burnings Are No Solution

McComb Enterprise-Journal,
Aug. 10

Negro Church Burned As Score Reaches 24

Delta Democrat-Times, Nov. 1

Church Blast Damage Called Rather Minor

Pascagoula-Moss Point
Chronicle, Sept. 11

Pike Officers 'Optimistic'

True Mission Spirit

The Mississippi Baptist Convention Board has announced that it will help collect funds to rebuild Negro churches which have burned this Summer.

We commend the Board. The action reflects the true mission spirit.

We believe in mission work—everywhere. And missions begin at home.

West Point **Times Leader,**
Aug. 13

A Pike County law officer reported today "we think there is some progress being made" in the investigation of two church burnings in this area within the past week.

Deputy Donald Dunn said "put that word 'THINK' in capital letters because we are not sure. But we seem to be getting some leads that may be valuable."

He added, "that's about all I can say about it now" but he did say there have been no arrests made in connection with the cases.

McComb **Enterprise-Journal,**
July 23

Negro Registration Ordered By Court

Meridian Star, July 11

Government Calls For Negro Registration

Delta Democrat-Times, Oct. 15

Voter Registration Wave For Mississippi Counties

Laurel Leader-Call, July 15

Maybe Lyndon Johnson and Martin Luther King will benefit, but mark this—America will profit nothing whatsoever.

God help the United States —she needs it.

Meridian Star, July 12

Will NAACP Have Jobs For All Negroes?

MERIDIAN STAR:

I noticed in the Meridian Star of June 28 some of the resolutions adopted by the N. A. A. C. P. at their recent national convention.

All of your race that I have talked to about this invasion of personal rights that we are facing have said, "I don't have anything to do with those people." Yet, some of you are involved in the invasion of personal rights.

Most seem to think, "I will sit astride the fence and if the Naps can get me something for nothing I will still be in their good graces for the grab; if not, nothing ventured, nothing lost."

What you are forgetting is that after all the steam has gone out of this foolishness, we all will have to have jobs. Will the Naps have jobs for all of you? Hardly. The leaders will have cleaned you for all you are worth and be vacationing in sunny Spain leaving the mess to be cleaned up by the remaining responsible citizens as was the case with their march on Washington. Did you see what a mess was made of our Capitol grounds?

Meridian Star, July 16

* A Mississippi newspaper columnist:
"It is foolish to believe that the architects of Mississippi's 'long hot summer' had as their objective the relatively innocent purpose of encouraging Negroes to vote"

The Grand Jury Friday attacked COFO's voter registration drive and asserted "There has never been any instance" when "qualified" Negroes were denied the right to vote in Jackson County.

"It was unanimously agreed upon by all who appeared that there has never been any instance where a Negro was refused the right to register and to vote if he was qualified," the report stated.

Pascagoula-Moss Point
Chronicle, July 19

"We went from house to house inviting Negroes to let us escort them to the courthouse to try to register. About 200 brave souls agreed to make the attempt, although they knew they would be subject to reprisals.

"We set out for the courthouse on a hot Thursday morning. By 9:30, the 200 Negroes were all lined up in a quiet file outside the courthouse.

"It was a long wait in the 95-degree sun. All benches had been removed from the courthouse grounds. The drinking water fountain for 'colored' had been disconnected, and the 'colored' bathroom was locked. After three hours, only three of them had gotten inside the courthouse

Grenada Sentinel-Star, Aug. 21

Canton, Mississippi: The long march to the courthouse to try to register to vote.

CORE

Entrance to a voter registration office

Cathy Amatniek

Mrs. Mary Robinson of Canton, a high school graduate active in voter registration work, told the court she had not attempted to register to vote before last February because "I'd heard colored people were turned away and never allowed to register."

Jackson Clarion-Ledger, Aug. 27

Another Negro, Charles Harris, a 38-year-old who received the "good conduct medal" and four battle stars while in the military service, testified he also was turned down because he was unable to interpret a section of the constitution to the registrar's satisfaction.

Jackson Clarion-Ledger, Aug. 27

Campbell testified that several ledgers dealing with voter registration and poll tax payment had been lost in a basement. When questioned by Judge Cox, he said there were "several books, perhaps 54 which were destroyed or misplaced" in a transfer to a courthouse basement.

Cecil Campbell, Sunflower
Circuit Clerk and Voter Registrar,
Jackson Clarion-Ledger, Aug. 27

The governor noted that between 27,000 and 30,000 Negroes are registered in Mississippi.

He said he knew of very few Negroes in the state who have been turned down for registration as voters and "very few instances, if any" of Negroes being intimidated by burnings, bombings and terroristic acts.

Delta Democrat-Times, Nov. 30

The latest figures on Negro voter registration released by the Southern Regional Council showed that only 6.7 per cent of eligible Negroes were registered in Mississippi. The figure compared with 67.2 per cent in Tennessee, another state in the old Confederacy.

Corinth Corinthian, Aug. 5

✳ There was a variety of opinion concerning voter registration

MERIDIAN STAR: After more than fifty y e a r s, the NAACP cause b e c a m e fashionable, a status symbol among liberals and some church groups. Political hearts began to bleed. When the Negro vote (even now they are registered like sheep) became the balance of power, a Civil Rights Act. was passed.

This nefarious, vicious and un-constitutional act must be repeal-ed. We have made this our most important goal.
"This may be our finest hour. We shall resist. we shall never surrender."

As one whose moral and fi-nancial support has helped so much in the past. we appeal to you for another contribution to this cause upon which depends our v e r y survival. Sincerely, ELLETT LAWRENCE(Finance Chairman, Association of Citizens Councils, Box 886, Greenwood, Miss.

Meridian Star, Oct. 17

THE lieutenant governor cited the fact that civil rights workers were "dedicated to registering Negroes to vote in Mississippi." He called for "an organized ef-fort to see that every white Mis-sissippian who is qualified is registered to vote before the next election."
Lt. Gov. Carroll Gartin,
Delta Democrat-Times, Dec. 9

"I forsee the danger of the Negroes, who are being urged by outsiders to register and vote, outstripping the voting strength of the white people if present apathy continues," Gar-tin said.
He urged the sheriffs, whom he described as closest to the people, to take up the fight to encourage all white people to register and vote.
Lt. Gov. Carroll Gartin,
Jackson **Clarion-Ledger**, Dec. 9

Tom Wakayama, SNCC

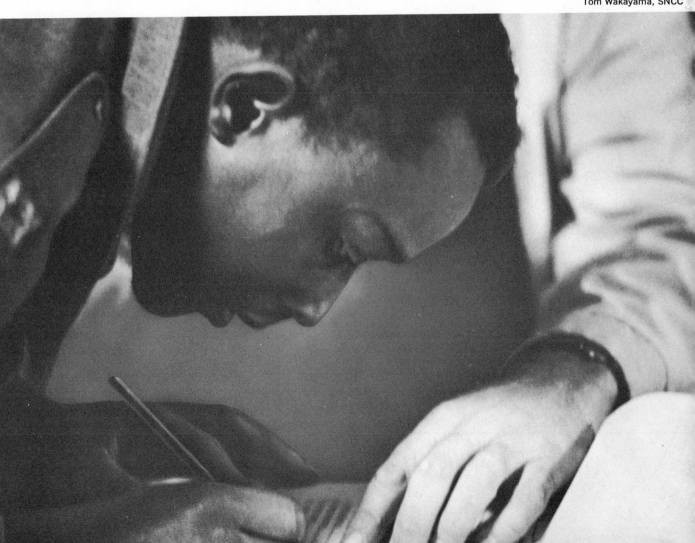

Ted Polumbaum

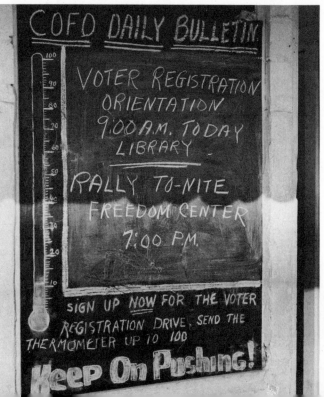

COFO DAILY BULLETIN

VOTER REGISTRATION
ORIENTATION
9:00 A.M. TODAY
LIBRARY

RALLY TO-NITE
FREEDOM CENTER
7:00 P.M.

SIGN UP NOW FOR THE VOTER
REGISTRATION DRIVE. SEND THE
THERMOMETER UP TO 100

Keep On Pushing!

Ed Hollander, CORE

92

Ted Polumbaum

✳ **Civil rights workers gave
voter instruction**

Ted Polumbaum

Tom Wakayama, SNCC

Court Testimony Reveals Illiterate White Voters

Delta Democrat-Times, Oct. 13

Madison County Clerk Denies Discrimination

Starkville News, Aug. 27

Dear Editor:

As reported in Drew Pearson's column, the Clarion-Ledger, August 5, a Negro congressman from California visiting Mississippi stated that a person must be highly educated before he can vote in this state.

This is just another of the untrue statements being made today about Mississippi. I, myself, not highly educated, having had only slight contact with college, can vote in Mississippi.

It is certainly to be regretted that such statements are made by persons who are able to determine the truth.

E. E. B.
Earle St.
Jackson, Miss.

Jackson **Clarion-Ledger**, Aug. 11

Behavior Said 'Shocking'

To The Editor:

You are receiving this letter from a private citizen of India.

Your (whites) shocking behavior toward the Negro only lets you down in the esteem of the rest of the world.

While your leaders, and people the world over, are striving for peace and goodwill amongst nations, you in your own country beget unrest and pour sorrow and suffering into the minds of those who are like you — people with mind soul and body. What a shame that there should be a struggle for freedom and justice amongst the people of so advanced a country as yours.

Why are Negroes in Mississippi denied the right to register to vote and why is it that Negro churches are regularly burned down?

Why is it that white jurors have seldom convicted a white man in a case involving a Negro?

It is with deep sorrow that we heard about the murder of three wonderful young civil rights workers in Mississippi. May there be an end to all this nonsense.

MRS. A. E.
Thilalenagar, India

Delta Democrat-Times, Sept. 17

Don't Destroy Your Freedom -- Keep It

MERIDIAN STAR: Open letter "TO THE COLORED PEOPLE OF MISSISSIPPI"; Have you ever taken the time to sit down and quietly think about your life in Mississippi? First, ask yourself, why do I live here? If I needed help, to whom would I go? And if I did ask, who would help me? I don't have to answer this for you. If you will be truthful to yourself you already know. And you also know, it wouldn't be the so-called do gooders from the North, who are supposedly here to help you. They couldn't care less what happens to you.

You also know that you are not being mistreated so why let these agitators make you believe you are.

You know yourself that you are treated as you treat others. This thing can bear a lot of thinking on your part, and if you will think back over the years, who have been the ones to give you a helping hand when you needed it most.

So, if you value freedom, then do something toward keeping the freedom you have, instead of completely destroying it yourselves.

F. R. T.
Collinsville, Miss.

Meridian Star, July 2

✱ A spokesman for the Southern Christian Leadership Conference said that at the present rate of registration, "it would take 135 years to register half of those eligible"

Tom Wakayama, SNCC

Neshoba County Negro Asserts Patience Tried By 'Bad Year'

Tupelo **Journal**, July 6

He said he has never attempted to register to vote. "But I'm going to one of these days."

Cole, who quit school after the seventh grade, said he had understood the three missing civil rights workers came into the community to aid Negroes.

"I feel like they came to help us," he said quietly. "Somebody's got to help us."

Tupelo **Journal**, July 6

One Negro man who lives within sight of a burned church he attended on the outskirts of historic Natchez, a city where shotgun houses border large estates with columned mansions, said he was not registered to vote and never expected to vote.

"I ain't interested in all that" said A. D. Bland, the father of five and the owner of five hound dogs. "I just don't know anything about voting."

Clarksdale Press Register,

July, 29

Those who
watched

Those who waited

Ted Polumbaum

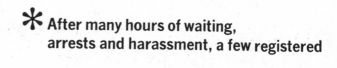
* After many hours of waiting, arrests and harassment, a few registered

Ted Polumbaum

Tom Wakayama, SNCC

GREENWOOD POL

Jailer's Wife Dispute Hunger Strike Claim

The Jackson County sheriff's department has a new Volkswagen prison wagon, delivered Tuesday, which will hold nine passengers.

In the recent arrests of 62 civil rights demonstrators in Pascagoula, a dilapidated prison bus and several station wagons were pressured into use to transport those arrested.

Biloxi-Gulfport **Herald**, Aug. 26

MERIDIAN, Miss., Dec. 1 — The Council of Federated Organizations claimed today one of its workers had staged a hunger strike in the Lauderdale County jail but the jailer's wife discounted the report.

A COFO spokesman said Sandra Watts, 22, of Lakeview, Ore., had not eaten since she was jailed Friday.

However, Mrs. Morris Myatt, the jailer's wife, said Miss Watts had eaten some but "was not cleaning up everything on her plate."

Tupelo **Journal**, Dec. 2

Over 100 Jailed After Greenwood Disturbance

Tupelo **Journal**, July 7

Pas Police Arrest 62 In Rally

Pascagoula-Moss Point
Chronicle, Aug. 5

Rights Worker Not 'Missing,' Found in Jail

McComb **Enterprise-Journal**,
July 7

Mayor Allen Thompson, of Jackson, has a favorite invitation he extends to visitors.

"Come enjoy our hospitality," he enjoins. "If you get in jail, I'll get you out. If I can't get you out, I'll get in there with you."

Jackson **Clarion-Ledger**,
Sept. 30

"An inspection of the City Jail and Police Station indicates a dire need for expansion," the report stated.

"We recommend that the expansion program now under way by the City as to the Police Station and the jail facilities be expedited."

Jackson **Clarion-Ledger**, July 10

In an elevator ride at the New Capitol, Wall inquired as to the whereabouts of the Hinds county jail.

"I'm going over there and see what they are doing to our people from my county," he snapped. "Why are the governor and the FBI running all over the place down our way arresting people and holding them in jail and not even letting them communicate with their folks?"

"The FBI and the Highway Patrol are harrassing our people to death and we want it stopped," Wall declared. "They let the COFO run around and cause all kinds of trouble, but you never hear about any of them getting arrested, just Mississippi people are going to jail."

Rep. Frank Wall, Amite County,
Jackson **Clarion-Ledger**, Oct. 9

* Jails overflowed with arrested courthouse pickets

Woman Uses Shotgun
Over Negroes Heads

Columbus **Commercial**
Dispatch, Aug. 16

GREENWOOD, Miss. (UPI)—
A white woman who operates a
store in the middle of a Negro
neighborhood fired a shotgun
into the air here Friday after a
group of 75-100 Negroes gath-
ered out front.

A spokesman for the Council
of Federated Organizations
(COFO) said Mrs. D e b b s
walked out in front of her store
"parading around with a shotgun and a crowd formed."
The spokesman claimed that
when Mrs. Debbs saw a white
civil rights worker across the
street taking her picture she
fired over his head.

Clarksdale Press Register,

Aug. 15

For some reason, it has become nationally popular to
damn Mississippi! But as more
and more visitors from other
states come to "inspect" this
"backward" state they are finding (much to their amazement)
an atmosphere which encour-
ages progress and prosperity.

West Point **Times Leader,**

July 7

The governor said Mississippians are to be congratulated
for acting the opposite to the
way others thought they would
act regarding the Civil Rights
Law.
Local leaders, he said, have
been successful in getting the
people to stand aside and let
law enforcement officers handle
the matter

Hattiesburg American, Aug. 17

Kenneth Thompson, NCC

✳ There were all types of intimidation

Canton Negro Says He's Being Pressured To Inform On Civil Rights Advocates

Clarksdale **Press Register,**
July 30

JACKSON. Miss. (UPI)— Negro grocer George Washington figured today his statements make him No. 1 on the Citizens Council's "agitator list" in his home town of Canton.

He said Canton city officials saw to it that numerous suppliers cut off his grocery store after he refused to evict a group of civil rights workers from one of his 25 rental houses and to tell them who attended mass meetings.

"Within a week 12 or 14 different distributors stopped calling on me," Washington said. He said the gasoline distributor came to me with tears in his eyes and said he was sorry, but he was going to' have to take my pumps."

Clarksdale **Press Register,**
July 30

Grocery Is Blown Up In Canton; Dynamite Found Under Another

Tupelo **Journal,** Sept. 7

Madison County authorities and FBI agents found several sticks of dynamite wrapped together under a grocery owned by George Washington, a Negro active in civil rights work in the rural county.

A can of explosives was also found atop his roof.

Laurel Leader-Call, Sept. 7

Kenneth Thompson, NCC

White Man In The South Is Now A Slave

Meridian Star, Aug. 10

MERIDIAN STAR: If slavery can be defined as involuntary servitude — and this seems a fair definition — then the position of the White man and the Black man in the South has been reversed.

Not since Civil War days has the Negro been compelled to work for anyone against his will under penalty of being imprisoned if he refused. But now under the provisions of the infamous public accommodations section of the new "Civil Rights" law, many Southern white men are compelled to serve those they don't want to serve, or face the penalty of imprisonment if they refuse.

Is this not a strange thing, that the grandsons of former slaves should be going over our land preaching that those who refuse to serve them should be imprisoned? It seems fair enough to say that any Negro — whether he has a "Rev." before his name, or not — who would send a white man to prison for refusing to serve him, publicly declares himself in favor of slavery.

No amount of preaching of injustices suffered by the Negroes of the South in times past can cover up these simple facts:

1. The white people of the South have also suffered injustices — and still do — and no one is trying to make amends to them.

2. Any Negro who does anything to send a white man to prison for refusing to serve him becomes guilty of the very thing he professes to abhor, forced servitude.

It seems that Southern white people, aided by our sensible colored people, must continue to take the lead in informing people throughout the nation in every way possible the evils of such a slave law. E. L. S.
RFD 1 Meridian.

Meridian Star, Aug. 10

Negro Schoolman's House, Car Damaged In Jackson Bomb Blast

Delta Democrat-Times, Sept. 28

Clifford Vaughs, SNCC

"We are at the real cross-roads—will the bombing of a barber shop, a newspaper office, an automobile, mark the beginning of unbridled lawlessness, or will we continue to hunt and prosecute criminals without fear or favor . . ."

Mayor Allen C. Thompson,
Jackson, Starkville News,
Sept. 29

More briefly, the Mississippi Negro knows that the Mississippi white man is his friend. And it works the other way around, too.

Starkville News, July 31

Dear Editor:

If we are really morally superior to these inferior, hate-filled, violent Negroes, let us prove it to others with our actions rather than to ourselves with our very audible conversation.

We must not let members of the Ku Klux Klan and their supporters prove to the nation what the liberal Northern press has been saying all along - that white Mississippians hate Negroes and would use the most despicable means to keep them in a position of servitude. And we must not let Jackson and Mississippi become examples of racial violence and hatred as have New York and New Jersey.

W.G. L.
424 Marshall,
Jackson
Jackson **Clarion-Ledger**, Aug. 20

Governor praises Negroes for keeping calm, harmony

Hattiesburg American, Aug. 11

✳ There was a variety of bombings across the state

Holly Springs Police Discount
Story COFO Workers Threatened

Tupelo **Journal**, July 2

Clifford Vaughs, SNCC

HOLLY SPRINGS — Mayor Sam Coopwood paid tribute to the Auxiliary policemen here saying that it was largely due to their effrots that racial trouble was avoided during the months of the summer project.

His statement follows:

"It is to be hoped that no one will get the impression that Holly Springs is a wild and wooley city because of the large number serving as policemen and auxiliary policemen. In fact, quite the contrary is true, for Holly Springs is a peaceful and law abiding city, remarkably free of crime and lawlessness over the years, and only a small city police force has been needed.

"Also in spite of a heavy colored population in Holly Springs, and Marshall County, there have been no racial disturbances since the Carpet Bag days, either in the city or county. The relationship of the two races over the years has been most amicable, and I can not recall a single instance where the racial issue has been involved in any disagreement coming before the city courts.

Jackson **Clarion-Ledger**, Oct. 27

Despite invasions by C O F O and others of similar ilk, this state has maintained law and order not matched by our Yankee critics anywhere.

Jackson **Clarion-Ledger**, Nov. 8

Fire Bomb
Planted?
It Seems So

Meridian Star, Sept. 2

103

Baptist College, Holly Springs

SHOOTING OF CR WORKER

Greenw'd has first CR arrest

Grenada **Sentinel-Star**, July 24

GREENWOOD, Miss. (AP)— The FBI has made its first arrests under the public accomodations sections of the new Civil Rights Act.

Agents of the bureau charged three Greenwood white men with a conspiracy designed to keep a Negro from going to a downtown movie theatre.

The FBI gave this report:

On July 16. McGhee staggered into the Greenwood FBI office. bleeding from head wounds and suffering from shock.

McGhee. a staff worker with the Student Non-Violent Coordinating Committee, said three men in a pickup truck forced him at the point of a gun to accompany them.

He said they asked him if he had been to the movie the previous night. When he replied yes he was beaten with a pipe and a board

Vicksburg **Post**, July 24

Two Greenwood men, T. A. Barrentine and Breland Ainsworth, signed property bonds and freed the three amid handshaking and back-slapping at the jail.

Grenada **Sentinel-Star**, July 24

Letters To The Editor

Greenwood **Commonwealth**, July 18

Dear Mr. Walt:

It was with some shock and disappointment that I read the account in your newspaper of the beating of two young men, on separate occasions, at the Leflore Theatre here in our own home town.

Obviously there were witnesses to the attack on this negro man by "a gang of white men." I would like to know if we are to expect attacks upon individuals by such hoodlums to follow this pattern in the future? I would like to know how many of these incidents will have to take place before someone is arrested or some serious attempt is made to investigate the matter?

Yours sincerely,
        Rev. L. D.
        Pastor.
        Immaculate Heart of
        Mary Church.

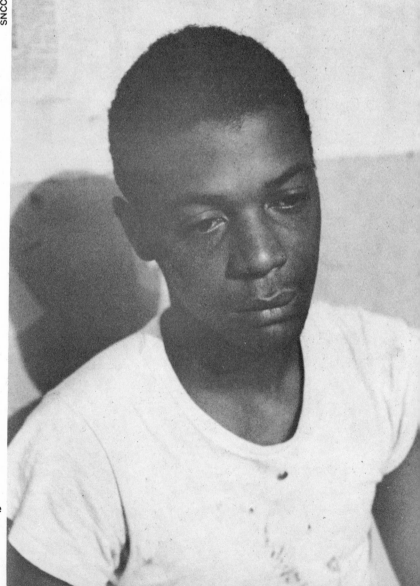

SNCC

Silas McGhee

SPARKS TENSION

Columbus **Commercial Dispatch**, Aug. 17

Negro Civil Rights Worker Shot In Face

Tupelo **Journal**, Aug. 17

Ross Praises Mississippi Law, Order

Jackson **Clarion-Ledger**, Aug. 21

Don't you ever get the idea that the industrialist and business men throughout this nation do not admire Mississippians for the stand that we have taken. They admire the people of Mississippi more than many people think. They like our attitudes, our fairness, our steadfastness and convictions.

Ex. Gov. Ross Barnett, **Natchez Democrat**, Dec. 1

* In Greenwood, a civil rights worker was shot in the face while sitting in a parked car, waiting for the rain to stop

Negro Youth Comes Home Where 'Things Are Peaceful'

VICKSBURG, Miss. (UPI) —A Negro youth who won acclaim in New York for rescuing a white boy from subway attackers, but wanted to return to Vicksburg, said Thursday he was home for good.

"I'm home to stay and I don't expect to go back," said Larry Thomas, 17. "I want to stay here where things are more peaceful."

Grenada **Sentinel-Star**, July 24

Anti-Mississippi Syndrome Is Baffling

Meridian Star, Aug. 15

MERIDIAN STAR: . . . THE PURE RACE MUST BE PRESERVED. (I presume you are of Norman stock?)

If so, we are behind you all the way, and any scapegoats you may think of in the meanwhile will be sincerely appreciated Heil,

    A. L.

    Meridian.

Meridian Star, July 10

Greenwood Civil Rights Workers Jump When A Car Passes

Delta Democrat-Times, Aug. 18

GREENWOOD (UPI) — The residents at 708 Ave. N. here jump every time a car passes.

THIS is the address of the national office of the Student Non - Violent Coordinating Committee (SNCC), and its biracial tenants are decidedly not welcomed by all the residents of this Delta City.

Robert Zellner, a young white SNCC field worker and a veteran of the civil rights struggle, was asked if the volunteer workers were jittery because of the Saturday shooting and wounding of a friend, Negro Silas McGhee.

"Yeah, it scares me to death," he said. "I was so jittery I got some horseshoes and went over to the community center and pitched some this afternoon."

Zellner stood talking to reporters outside the building. A 100-watt light bulb lit the front yard at 708 and its residents, including five or six young white college students from the North and a group of local Negroes.

Every time a car passed, everyone jumped behind the SNCC staff cars, four light-colored new vehicles with long whip antennas which were parked out front.

"That's a white," Zellner said. "Get the number." There was no license tag.

At this time, a city police car with four helmeted police officers inside drove up. Zellner ran to it and said "There goes a suspicious pickup. It doesn't have any tag and there are two whites in it."

The police car pulled off, but did not follow the truck.

Every night the hide-and-seek goes on. Every car that drives by means a potential bomb.

"You aren't any safer inside," Zellner said. "They could toss a bomb through the window." . . .

Delta Democrat-Times, Aug. 18

Civil Rights Workers In Shaw Are Undaunted By Bomb Threat

Delta Democrat-Times, July 16

Matt Herron

GULFPORT, Miss (AP)— Harrison County supervisors are considering a program to get rid of pigeons and sparrows on the courthouse and other public buildings.

A pest control company agent says it can be done through a scientific "scare" program with guaranteed results.

McComb Enterprise-Journal, Nov. 10

Mayor Charles Dorrough of Ruleville, Miss.

Perhaps Mayor Charles Dorrough of Ruleville, president of the Mississippi Municipal Association, summed it up best:

"Our big job now is to clean up the state's image, splattered by the rights workers. We'll now have to teach the younger Negroes the Democratic and Christian way of doing things."

Jackson **Clarion-Ledger**, Aug 16

Dorrough expressed pleasure at the resolution adopted.

The resolution urged the civil rights workers coming into the state to "go immediately to the chief of police of the town or city in which they are located and register in order that precautions may be taken by local officials in their behalf."

Jackson **Clarion-Ledger**, July 1

* **Mayor Charles Sampson of Greenwood: "We haven't had too much racial trouble here this summer"**

107

Officers Seek Clues To Vicksburg Bombing

Natchez Democrat, Oct. 5

VICKSBURG, (AP) — Federal agents sifted for clues Sunday to the latest Mississippi night bombing in the water-soaked wreckage of a house used as headquarters by a civil rights organization.

The rear of the two-story "Freedom School" of the Council of Federated Organizations — COFO — was demolished by a 2:48 a.m. blast.

Officers said the explosive apparently was placed under the rear of the building. It demolished three bedrooms, the kitchen and some 9,000 books in COFO's "Freedom Library."

Debris was hurled 100 yards from the blast.

Jackson **Clarion-Ledger**, Oct. 5

Reply From Vicksburg

Jackson **Clarion-Ledger**, Nov. 5

"I never have condoned the presence, actions or activities of the COFO workers in Vicksburg," Mayor John D. Holland of Vicksburg said Saturday in a statement.

"Drew Pearson's column printed last Thursday in The Clarion-Ledger quoted me in such a way as to infer that I was condoning the actions of COFO workers in the Vicksburg area," Mayor Holland declared.

"It gives the impression that I might condone their work, but I don't condone their presence, actions or activities here," the Mayor emphasized "Any implications otherwise are purely erroneous. I never said they were good kids, or anything complementary."

Vicksburg Post, Oct. 18

Clifford Vaughs, SNCC

Freedom House, Vicksburg

Gov. Johnson Tells Nation Racial Troubles Being 'Resolved Fairly'

Tupelo **Journal,** Dec. 1

Clifford Vaughs, SNCC

Mrs. Louise Brown

Injured in the blast were Mrs. Louise Brown and her two-month-old grandson, Hank.

Besides Mrs. Brown and her grandson, occupants of the house were Mrs. Brown's children: Sandra 15, the boy's mother; Carl Louis, 18; Linda, 11; Audrey Elaine, 10; Kit Lamar, 4; and Jacqueline, 3; white COFO workers Elaine Singer, 20 Endicott, N.Y.; Emily Gordon, 28, Ann Arbor, Mich.; and Bryan Dunlap, 20, Leonia, N.J.; and Vicksburg Negroes Henry Coleman, 19; J. C. Hayes 20; and Henry Hunter, 19.

Vicksburg Post, Oct. 5

Mrs. Brown said, "I don't know where I'll go now. My relatives are afraid to take me in." She has six children all of whom were in the house.

Vicksburg Post, Oct. 5

✳ Mayor John P. Holland of Vicksburg: "I don't like the COFO or any of these liberals. To me they are a stinking lot and I mean just that"

Mayor R. B. Meadows of Gulfport said his city had no segregation ordinances.

"Regardless of the federal civil rights law," he said, "in a reasonable period of time we would have solved our problems due to the work of leaders of both races who have gone on the proposition that people of good will on both sides of the question can work out the solution."

Laurel Leader-Call, Oct. 22

Dear Editor:

On this earth God has placed man, and man has brought up certain principles and issues by which he lives. And during the course of time, these principles and these issues h a v e caused man to make war and to make peace, and to love and to hate.

Again we are faced with a situation in which man is earnestly managing to create hatred. This civil rights issue — naturaly there is a pro and a con force facing it, just l i k e there is a pro and a con force for every issue brought up on this earth.

We as Southerners will fight against the civil rights bill w h i l e the Northerners will fight for it (generally speaking, that is). But we shall make no headway other than to hurt ourselves if we don't sit down and think about this.

I have done this—and now I know I'm right.

D. S.
Provine High '65,
Jackson, Miss.

Jackson **Clarion-Ledger,** July 8

Collins man charged with beating of Ohio rabbi

Hattiesburg American, July 18

UPI

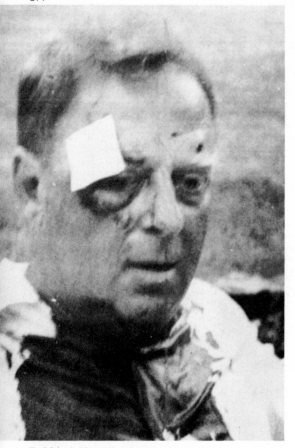

Rabbi Arthur Lelyveld

Maximum penalty on conviction of assault and battery with intent to maim is 10 years.

Hattiesburg American, July 18

✳ **In Hattiesburg an out-of-state rabbi and two COFO workers were bludgeoned**

Rabbi Says He's Sorry For Mississippi People

Rabbi Arthur Lelyveld, 51, of Cleveland, Ohio, said he feels "only pity" for the two white men who beat him and his companions, Lawrence D. Spears, 21, of Palo Alto, Calif., and David Owen, 19, of Pasadena, Calif.

But he added that he has "profound admiration for what I have seen in the Negro community here."

"I have found friendliness, hospitality and gentleness along penury in which so many (Negroes) live," he said.

"It is pitiful that the leaders of the state fall to realize that they are shaping their own doom along with that of the closed society they have created," Lelyveld said.

Pascagoula-Moss Point
Chronicle, July 12

Pair fined in beating of rabbi

Clifton Archie Keys, 51, and his 31-year-old nephew Kilmer Estus Keys, both of Covington County, entered pleas of nolo contendere in County Court today and each was fined $500 on a charge of assault and battery. The charge stemmed from the July 10 beating here of a civil rights worker, Rabbi Arthur Lelyveld of Cleveland. O.

Judge William Haralson also sentenced each man to 90 days in jail but time was suspended on condition of good behavior.

Hattiesburg American, Aug. 8

To listen to the T.V. statesmen, one would think that Mississippi was in a state of riot, bloodshed, and lawlessness, that we went around knocking people in the head with a baseball bat, or slashed their throats with a crabapple switch. It is most amazing for me to sit here quietly in my home in peaceful little Rosedale and hear the things they say.

Jackson **Clarion-Ledger,** July 5

Police were also investigating a report from another summer volunteer, Philip Hocker, 19, a Princeton student of Corning, N.Y. who said he was beaten with a baseball bat by a white man across the street from the COFO headquarters in a Negro section near here.

Hocker said he was hit on the back of the head with the bat, knocked down and hit several other times before the white man ran.

Hocker was taken to a local hospital and treated in the emergency room.

Tupelo **Journal,** Aug. 17

Ed Hollander, CORE

Mississippi landscape

Mississippi Is The Best Place To Live

MERIDIAN STAR: Many horrible things have been said about Mississippi and its people, but take it from one who has lived here since birth, I think it is the very best place to live on earth. It's a place where people will speak to you and greet you with "HOW ARE YOU ALL." It's a place that will live in one's memory and stand so very tall. It's a place where the people are happy. COFO and the NAACP are not needed at all. Let them go clean up around their own door. If we need them we will give them a call. Here in Mississippi you can listen to the mocking birds sing in the evening and at night you can hear the whippoorwill's lonely call. Here in Mississippi we produce the friendliest people of all. It's a place where we practice God's will in segregation. It's the "Garden Spot" of all God's creation.

In the Miss America pageant our own Mary Ann and Linda Lee took the show. As a state that produces beautiful women you have no further to go.

So I prefer to live in Mississippi where freedom reigns supreme. Beautiful Mississippi, land of my dreams. Thank you.

R. H.
Route 7, Meridian.

Meridian Star, Aug. 23

Negro Says Cop 'Deodorized' Her

McComb **Enterprise-Journal**, Sept. 24

FULL FAITH

The strange thing is that while everyone sees violence and bloodshed in the South, we folks who live here have never been witness.

Never have we seen a woman insulted on the streets of a Mississippi city or town, much less stripped of her clothing and raped.

Never have weeen a woman chased down a street and slashed to death.

These and many other things we hear about, have never happened in Mississippi.

Yet we stand accused. . .the whitest people in the world. . . .

Jackson **Clarion-Ledger**, July 12

"But it is also clear that the solution of the problems, particularly those brought on by racial differences, can only be found through the efforts of local citizens, with local control and local adjustments. These problems are not capable of solution by placing them in the hands of the federal government or under some rigid federal formula. Insofar as law enforcement is concerned, it is clear that law enforcement must be left in the hands of local authorities."

Pascagoula-Moss Point
Chronicle, Nov. 12

Sheriffs For Peace

Jackson **Clarion-Ledger**, Dec. 13

Steve Schapiro

The bearers of gossip are surely having a field day. The air is filled with rumors, reports accusations and alleged incidents. In most cases these reports are entirely figment of the imagination and in all cases the reports are the product of much exaggeration.

For instance: I have been hearing for several days that the City Police shot and killed somebody; who, nobody knows — they just heard it. Nobody knows anything about it, but many have passed the report on, adding their own little bit to it and it is making the rounds over the community.

The actual facts are that not one of the city police has fired a gun at anyone — there has been no incident that would lend itself even remotely to violence.

Grenada Sentinel Star, Aug. 10

Expanded State Police Powers Little Used In 'Long Summer'

Tupelo Journal, Aug. 14

On Saturday August 22, at about 5 in the afternoon, 15 white men, armed with pistols and rifles, clubs and chains attacked a group of four COFO workers and several local Negroes on the Currie farm, about five miles southwest of Laurel. One of the white COFO workers, Dave Gelfand a Brandies student from White Plains, New York was hospitalized overnight with injuries to his back, knee and wrist.

They were sitting near the pond, singing folk songs, when two white men appeared, one carrying a chain and the other carrying a wooden club. The men ordered Gelfand to play "Dixie" on the guitar, and even though he did not know the song, he tried to learn. One of the men grabbed the guitar and threw it into the pond. He then started to beat Gelfand.

Both Gelfand and Hayden jumped into the pond and swam under water to the other side. The others ran towards the farm house. By this time, 13 more whites had appeared around the pond, and several fired at the swimming COFO workers while others fired at the farmhouse.

When they reached the other side, Hayden was able to run to the house under cover of fire that by this time was being returned from the house. Gelfand, however, was seized again and beaten further. He was finally able to escape to the house.

...During the shooting, both the Laurel police and the Jones county sheriff were called.

The sheriff arrived an hour later, took a brief account of what had happened and took down all our names. When we requested that he follow us back to Laurel, his reply was, "I didn't carry you out here." He did not search the area.

Laurel Leader-Call, Aug. 24

Peter Werner of Flint, Mich., a civil rights worker in Hattiesburg

Herbert Randall

White Civil Righter Is Struck By Hattiesburg Man

HATTIESBURG, Miss. (UPI) — A local resident struck a white civil rights worker in the downtown area Monday and both men were arrested by police.

Charged with assault and battery were Peter Werner of Flint, Mich., and Houston Hartfield of Hattiesburg. They were released on $25 bond.

Meridian Star, July 12

* **Governor Johnson announced the training of 3,000 auxiliary state policemen**

Former Adams Sheriff Ired by Patrol Search

McComb Enterprise-Journal, Oct. 1

City Has No Control Over State Patrolmen

Natchez Democrat, Nov. 11

Mayor John J. Nosser yesterday stated that in connection with the stationing of the Mississippi Highway Safety Patrol members and investigators in Natchez and Adams County in an effort to solve bombings, shootings, beatings and the like over the past several months and to prosecute those guilty, he would like to issue the following statement:

"Investigation revealed that finances were not available to employ sufficient policemen and deputy sheriffs to solve the incidents in Natchez and Adams County and preserve law and order. It was then that a conference was held between the Governor, Chief of Police, Sheriff, and Mayor and it was decided to have Governor Johnson send the Highway Patrol and its investigators to Natchez and Adams County to work with local officers to solve the acts of violence and restore peace and order.

"We did not want federal troops sent to Natchez and Adams County and for that reason we decided to have the Highway Patrol sent in to help.

"After this agreement was reached, the local officers had and have no control over the methods used by the Highway Patrol and their investigators in their investigations here. The control rests solely in the hands of the Governor.

"It is my belief that if the Highway Patrol is withdrawn and there are future incidents that federal troops will be moved into Natchez and Adams County and this should certainly be avoided."

Natchez Democrat, Nov. 12

Natchez, Mississippi
Gentlemen:

Recent events in Natchez and Adams County certainly have called for some stringent law enforcement by our local Police and the Sheriff's Department.

The Governor of the State of Mississippi, according to our information, sent some 50 Highway Patrolmen into our area to assist in apprehending persons who have caused property damage by bombings.

However, according to our information and whereas the desire of our Governor may have been most worthy, we find that he did not follow the Mississippi law which authorizes the Highway Patrol to exercise general police powers from information received from the office of the Secretary of the State of Mississippi, we have been advised that the Governor did not issue a proclamation in invoking the power and authority vested in the Highway Patrol under the Acts of the 1964 Regular Legislative Session.

Under House Bill No. 564 of the Regular Legislative Session of 1964, the Department of Public Safety, upon the signing of a proclamation by the Governor, is authorized to exercise additional powers throughout certain areas, which powers are, in effect, general police powers. The Act provides that when such proclamations are issued by the Governor or Acting Governor, the same shall be filed with the Office of the Secretary of State on the next succeeding business day.

It would thus appear that for the past several weeks our citizens have been subjected to unnecessary harassment by officers in our Highway Patrol acting without legal authority.

We ask that you call the above discrepancy to the attention of our Governor and ask that he invoke a proclamation and make same public if he intends to continue with his indiscriminate apprehension or arrest of our citizens in Natchez and Adams County.

The Governor's attention suld be directed also to the fact that many of our citizens are being deprived of their constituional righ by unreasonable searches and seizures. Many guns carried by our citizens are properly carried under our Constitution and have been seized by the Mississippi Highway Patrol. Upon demands, the Highway Patrol and local officials have refused to restore to the individuals concerned their weapons. We would remind you that European dictators were they were able to seize local weapons and thus subdue the people.

Please call to our Governor's attenton our complaints and let me assure you of our full cooperation in restoring law and order to Natchez and Adams County.

Very truly yours,
Chairman, Natchez Chapter
AMERICANS FOR THE PRESERVATION OF THE WHITE RACE, INC.

Natchez Democrat, Nov. 6

STRONG PROTESTS have been voiced by Natchez civic groups and individuals against what they regard as illegal searches by FBI agents and state highway patrolmen, allegedly acting without proper warrants.

HISTORY MAY show that the most flagrant violations of the 4th Amendment were committed by the federal government during the illegal and tyrannical military invasion of Mississippi by the Kennedy regime.

Masterminding this rape of the Constitution was our present U. S. Attorney General, Nicholas Katzenback, who appointed himself as a sort of federal dean at the University of Mississippi. . .

HAVING SHOWN such callous disregard for the constitutional rights of Mississippians then, it is not very surprising that Comrade Katzenback (isn't that a Russian name?) has evidently chosen to ignore the protests of Natchez citizens regarding allegedly illegal searches by federal and state agents in recent weeks.

Jackson Clarion-Ledger, Nov. 19

BOMB BLASTS HOME OF NATCHEZ MAYOR

Laurel Leader-Call, Sept. 26

White Terrorists Suspected Of Bombing Natchez Mayor

Delta Democrat-Times, Sept. 27

'Stink Bombs' Hurled At Natchez Businesses

Pascagoula-Moss Point Chronicle, Sept. 15

Fifth Natchez Man Is Arrested for Beating

McComb Enterprise-Journal, Oct. 23

Natchez Statement Asks 'Peace, Responsibility'

McComb Enterprise-Journal, Oct. 18

✳ Governor Johnson moved the highway patrol into Natchez — a particular troublesome spot

Governor Johnson Appeals To Natchez People To Give Aid

Natchez Democrat, Oct. 3

$5000.00
REWARD

The Mayor And Board of Aldermen are vitally concerned about the many incidents of bombings, lawlessness and destruction of private property that have occurred in our fair city. Natchez is a tourist resort and an industrial area and depends heavily upon the income and patronage of tourists and industries that come into this area, and it is essential that we have an atmosphere in our city that is conducive to peace, trade, and business development. Many of our citizens have been threatened with bodily harm and property destruction. Under these circumstances we do not know when, where or whom the terrorists will strike next. Therefore, it behooves every law-abiding citizen to cooperate with the local authorities in assuring that these acts of violence will not be repeated.

FAILURE OF ANY CITIZEN TO ACT WOULD HAVE JUST AS DRASTIC A RESULT AS COOPERATING WITH THE PERSONS WHO ARE COMMITTING THE ACTS OF VIOLENCE.

Thus, the Mayor and Board of Aldermen do appeal to the citizens of Natchez and all of the civic organizations and clubs in the city for their full co-operation in reporting any unlawful incident and furnishing to the city authorities any information that would lead to the apprehension of those undesirable citizens who are determined to cause unrest and ill-feeling in our community by the destruction of private property and by threatening to do bodily violence to those who stand in their way.

The Mayor and Board feel that it is necessary that a reward be offered and do, therefore, offer for a period of 90 days from date the sum of $5,000.00 for evidence leading and substantially contributing to the arrest and conviction of the person or persons guilty of the unlawful acts of violence, bombing of buildings, homes or other establishments within the City Of Natchez.

Sincerely,

MAYOR

And

BOARD OF ALDERMEN

Advertisement, **Natchez Democrat**, Sept. 16

The Peoples'
FORUM

NOTICE OF BOMBING

Dear Fellow Citizens-

Last Sunday night (September 13) at 11:40 pm a bomb was thrown at our home at 400 Cedar Street in Vidalia. My wife, Tammy, and I rushed outside to see where in Vidalia or Natchez it was, and to spot any fire. It was not until daylight that we discovered a singed hole in our own front yard and bomb scraps all over the automobile and carport. Who would bomb us?

Since I am a theoretic and practicing segregationist, with malice toward none, and charity for all, I cannot hang on to any ideas that the "Klan" did the bombing — at least on THAT account. Since I am active in absolutely no organization but the Cub Scouts, I cannot believe that the "Klan". . . etc. Since my great, great, grandfather was a genuine Virginia Colonel and among the real people who built the South, Constitution Bill of Rights, etc., I cannot believe the "Klan". . . etc.

Unless someone was just throwing away an extra bomb as they passed our house, there could be no reason to bomb me. The only possible motive I cannot toally disregard is that privately I am known as an intense "pro-union man", have taken Jack Kennedy as a personal hero, and support President Johnson and the Democrat Party as the best hope for America, the South, and especially the workingman.

The few very close friends I talk to know me as basically a quiet scholar who spends most of his spare time working around hhe house and reading on grammar and history, which I teach in school. Only a horrendous fear and disrespect of law and order could bring such terrible violence to us and our four kids because of my private political beliefs. (I have even given heartfelt encouragement to some Republicans in favor of a two-party system).

With all the known violence of late and long, only Gov. Paul Johnson of Mississippi and Mayor John Nosser of Natchez have spoken against thuggery. Our policemen have become outnumbered, outgunned, and outsmarted by the organized terrorists who know the difficulty of obtaining clues and witnesses. In fact, the Mississippi River cannot carry as much water as the vitriol spilled out by our local newspapers and public officials against the United States Government and the loyal Democratic Party.

I see no good advice for any of us except 'The Sermon on the Mount".

Thank you,
B.D.

Natchez Democrat, Sept. 20

* **A $5,000 reward was posted by Mayor Nosser of Natchez**

RACIAL VIOLENCE HIGH IN McCOMB

Laurel Leader-Call, Sept. 21

Dynamite Rips Negro Home, Church in City

McComb Enterprise-Journal, Sept. 21

Variety of Officers Study City 'Bombings'

McComb Enterprise-Journal, Sept. 22

* McComb – in Pike county –
in Southwest Mississippi
was a
particular trouble spot

Sheriff Calls McComb Bombing 'Plant'

Natchez Democrat, Sept. 22

Bombings In McComb Come During Quiet Night Hours

Meridian Star, Oct. 2

8th 'Bombing' Contains Several Unusual Aspects

McComb **Enterprise-Journal**, Aug. 28

McComb's Police Chief Discusses Difficulty Of Coping With Bombs

Jackson **Clarion-Ledger**, Sept. 30

'Peculiar' Circumstances Surround McComb Blasts

Jackson **Clarion-Ledger**, Sept. 25

City Police Had Very Busy Month

McComb **Enterprise-Journal** Sept. 28

Officers on Run in Racial Affairs

McComb **Enterprise-Journal**, Aug. 17

What Is Frightening People of McComb?

McComb **Enterprise-Journal**, Oct. 28

$5,000

in cash rewards

(1) $2,500 in cash will be paid for information leading to the arrest and conviction of the person or persons responsible for any of the 1964 bombings of property in Pike County, Mississippi.

(2) Cash in varying amounts will also be paid from a separate fund in excess of $2,500 for any accurate and useful information regarding plans for future or past bombings.

Any person or persons desiring to apply for the $2,500 cash reward or to claim payment from the separate fund for useful and accurate information should immediately contact Sheriff R. R. Warren or any licensed attorney-at-law practicing in Pike County.

These reward funds and the funds for this publication are being supplied by the private citizens of Pike County in keeping with the spirit of the previously published statement of the Mayor and Board of Selectmen of the City of McComb City directed to the maintenance of law and order. Said statement has been publicly endorsed by the directors of the McComb Chamber of Commerce, the McComb Rotary Club, the McComb Lions Club, the McComb Exchange Club, the Jaycees and others.

We are no longer dealing with a question of segregation. We are faced with the definite possibility that the life of this community is at stake.

Any person or persons desiring to contribute to these funds should make his contribution directly or anonymously by mailing the contribution to Private Citizens Reward Fund, % Sheriff R. R. Warren, Magnolia, Mississippi.

Money received in excess of the amounts needed for these purposes will be refunded on a prorata basis to known contributors.

Contributions large or small, and the assistance of the public are earnestly solicited. You can mail check or currency.

This reward notice paid for by the contributions of private citizens of Pike County through Sheriff R. R. Warren is now in effect.

$5,000

Clifford Vaughs, SNCC

Society Hill Baptist Church, McComb, Miss.

✳ Sixteen bombings in a matter of weeks occurred in Pike county and McComb

ROUND The WORLD For JESUS

*H*ow far are YOU willing to go? A little way? Half way? Completely around the world??? Have YOU ever heard His command, "Go ye into all the world...?" Well, what are you doing about it? Have you answered that call? *This is the moment of decision.* It is a personal decision... a positive act of the will. It must be performed in the lonely solitude of your soul, in the presence of its Maker. *Then, Choose YE this day.* Decide right now just how far YOU are ready to go for Him. Gilder said, "As for me and my house, if Jesus Christ were a man and only a man, I say that of all mankind I would cleave to Him, and to Him would I cleave alway. But if Jesus Christ is God and the very God, I vow I will follow Him through Heaven and Hell, the Earth, and Sea, and Air!" How far will you go???

Advertisement, Columbus **Commercial Dispatch**, Dec. 6

121

Heffners' Claim of Being

Mother Of Former 'Miss Mississippi' Says Family Forced Out Of McComb

Meridian Star, Sept. 6

JACKSON, Miss. (AP) — The Albert Heffner family, parents of Miss Jan Nave, Miss Mississippi of 1963, left their ten-year home at McComb in South Mississippi because of what they called "unbelievable threats and intimidations." The mother of the past Miss Mississippi weaved a shocking tale Saturday explaining how her family was "run out" of their hometown because they associated with several civil rights workers.

Meridian Star, Sept. 6

Mrs. Albert Heffner told a news conference here the "series" of incidents began two months ago because she and her husband sought to "establish communications" between law officers in the southwest Mississippi town and civil rights workers involved in the Mississippi summer project.

Tupelo Journal, Sept. 7

Albert Heffner, lay reader, Protestant Episcopal church, McComb, Miss.
Mrs. Heffner, far left
Miss Jan Nave, Miss Mississippi of 1963, Mrs. Heffner's daughter by a former marriage.

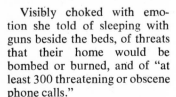
UPI

UPI

Visibly choked with emotion she told of sleeping with guns beside the beds, of threats that their home would be bombed or burned, and of "at least 300 threatening or obscene phone calls."

"The fear was almost unbearable," she related. "One night when the highway patrol was watching the house we had to hide out at the Holiday Inn. The FBI told us not to leave the room for anything."

She said her daughter's three pets had been killed, and that when her daughter, Carla, 17, returned from a trip to New York she was repeatedly threatened and insulted.

"When I'd go downtown, people I had known all my life would treat me like I had leprosy. We just couldn't ask Carla to live in that atmosphere."

Meridian Star, Sept. 6

* There was harassment of those who tried to build a bridge between the civil rights workers and the white community

Don McCord

Hounded From City Spreads

Harrassed Heffners Recite Tale Of Tension, Terror In McComb

Delta Democrat-Times, Sept. 9

Albert W. (Red) Heffner Jr. of 202 Shannon Dr. issued a statement today in connection with reports that he had entertained two civil rights workers in his home Friday evening.

Heffner said, it is true that two white civil rights workers were in my home on this evening. But it was a conference and not a matter of entertainment. The purpose of the conference was to let the civil rights workers hear the Mississippi point of view.

"Nothing was done in my home or elsewhere which was not fully disclosed to law enforcement authorities at the time. I have worked closely with the authorities for the best interests of our town and state. I shall always work to this end for each and every member of my family is a native Mississippian, dedicated to the best interest of our people."

McComb Enterprise-Journal, July 22

MRS. HEFFNER recalled with obvious terror the day she found out that her house was supposed to have been bombed the preceding night.

I learned about it while I was swimming at a motel pool. But I soon found out that I was about the only one in my neighborhood who didn't know about it," she said.

"A four-year-old child came up to me and asked, 'When is your house going to be bombed?'"

Delta Democrat-Times, Sept. 9

Mayor Says Heffners Asked No Assistance

Jackson Clarion-Ledger, Sept. 8

The city's mayor, Gordon Burt Jr., said the Heffner family never appealed to the city for assistance.

"It looks to me like Mrs. Heffner has made some observations and conclusions which she had not carefully considered before making them," Burt said when informed of her statements.

EDITOR'S NOTE: **The following article appeared in the Sept. 13 edition of "The Everyday Magazine" in the St. Louis Post-Dispatch.**

He could not see it then, but Red Heffner took the first step on his road to ruin on July 7, five days after President Lyndon B. Johnson signed the Civil Rights Act.

In a move to establish communication between the races, he got in touch with two Negro business acquaintances and offered his services as a go-between to the white community in case of violence. He informed Police Chief George Guy of what he had done and promised to keep Guy posted.

...The Heffners are pure Mississippi. They look it, they sound it, they feel it.

Heffner, who is known as Red, was born 42 years ago in Greenwood, Miss., and was reared on a plantation. He traces his Mississippi ancestry back three generations. His great-grandfather was a Confederate army officer.

"I had no idea that anything like this was going on."

He added, "perhaps there are some differences in our basic attitudes with civil rights workers and they have never been welcome in McComb, but if the Heffners were threatened and intimidated, if they had spoken up, they might have been assisted."

Biloxi-Gulfport Herald, Sept. 7

Heffner's wife, Malva, daughter of an attorney, also was reared on a plantation. Her family goes back even further into Mississippi history, having settled in the area before it became a state.

In 1957 Heffner received a community service award from the McComb Chamber of Commerce. He is a lay reader in the Protestant Episcopal Church. He is a past president of the Mississippi Multiple Sclerosis Association and of the Pike County Little Theater Association. He was an organizer of the Pike County Association for Exceptional Children. His insurance firm gave him an award for an outstanding sales record in 1963.

Mrs. Heffner, 40, was president of the McComb Youth Center Association and was instrumental in raising $30,000 to build the city's first youth center. The project took six years. She also was vice president of the McComb Recreation Committee and was a member of the Junior Auxiliary for five years.

McComb Enterprise-Journal, Sept. 16

Alyene Quin

Mrs. Charles Bryant

Mrs. Willie J. Dillon

Clifford Vaughs, SNCC

Clifford Vaughs, SNCC

McComb Negro mothers are on way to Washington to seek protection

Hattiesburg American, Sept. 22

A bomb wrecked Mrs. Quin's home Sunday night. Her two children were slightly hurt and a babysitter escaped injury.

"I've no place to stay," she said. "Everyone's afraid to have me in their house now. I don't even know where my children are staying at this moment."

She told a news conference that FBI agents are in McComb "but they work with the local police . . . and not one person has been arrested."

Mrs. Dillon said her home has been bombed, her children threatened and her husband has been in jail for three weeks "because he worked on a COFO car."

She explained that her·husband, a mechanic, had been charged with operating an unlicensed garage "when he doesn't even have a garage."

Mrs. Bryant said she doesn't know what is going to happen in the McComb area "but I know it won't be good."

She said that "from what we see, the city police are on the spot before the smoke is settled from the bombings. They must know where the bombings are going to be."

Laurel Leader-Call, Sept. 23

In Washington since Tuesday were Alyene Quinn, whose home was bombed Sunday night; Mrs. Willie J. Dillon, whose home was bombed Aug. 28, and Mrs. Charles Bryant, whose home was bombed July 27.

Tupelo Journal, Sept. 25

President Johnson has asked the Justice Department for a prompt investigation of a number of bombings in McComb, Miss.

The President told three Negro women from McComb in a White House meeting Thursday that he was deeply concerned by the bombing of Negro homes, churches and other buildings in the southwest Mississippi town.

Corinth Corinthian, Sept. 25

124

Blast, COFO Liquor Raid,
Crosses Feature Weekend

McComb **Enterprise-Journal**, Aug. 17

"COFO has no authority with state, local nor any other honest government," Johnson said.

"No city would send to Washington as a representative any woman whose criminal record is as long as the Illinois Central railroad," he asserted.

The governor apparently referred to a recent trip made to the White House by a McComb woman seeking audience with the President about happenings in McComb.

"In my opinion, the good people will rise up and stop all of this," Johnson said. "The good Negroes of the area and all over the state can help too by bringing information to the proper authorities.

Gov. Paul Johnson,
Jackson **Clarion-Ledger**, Oct. 1

Negro Police Says Quit Force In McComb When Asked To 'Spy'

Natchez Democrat, Sept. 27

Former Negro Policeman Testifies; Home Bombed

Pascagoula-Moss Point
Chronicle, Sept. 24

"I have never been notified by a colored person on one of these bombings," the Pike County sheriff said Friday. "Instead the calls have gone directly to the FBI, COFO (the Council of Federated Organizations) or to some other agency.

Vicksburg Post, Sept. 26

Johnson agreed with local officials that some of the bombings appeared to be "plants" by civil rights workers to gain support for their activities.

Gov. Paul Johnson,
Corinth **Corinthian**, Oct. 1

Sheriff Warren said he felt the press hadn't given his officers or the people of Mississippi a "fair shake" in reporting the news from McComb.

"We're having a heck of a time getting our side of the story across," the sheriff said.

McComb **Enterprise-Journal**,
Oct. 29

When asked how great tensions are in the area, Mayor Burt said "it is difficult to measure tension" but admitted tensions have grown "this summer since the COFO workers came here."

McComb **Enterprise-Journal**,
Sept. 22

The seventh apparent "bombing" of McComb's summer wave of racial activities was but one of a number of spectacular events over the past weekend.

A blast of undetermined nature shattered most windows and tore up a metal canopy at a two-story concrete block building at Warren and Denwiddie Streets early Saturday:

Officers of the forces of Sheriff R. R. Warren and Chief of Police George Guy combined early Sunday to raid two COFO occupied houses in Burglund in a futile search for illegal liquor.

At least three fiery crosses blazed, at Osyka, Chatawa and Magnolia.

Police were hard pressed to keep down what might have turned into a disastrous riot at the scene of the blast that shook up the Burglund Super Market — Eureka Masonic lodge building.

And, although it had nothing to do with racial activities and will be described in a separate story, a young McComb Negro killed himself in what was called a game of "Russian roulette" with a .22 revolver.

McComb **Enterprise-Journal**,
Aug. 17

*Negro mothers — victims of bombings — petitioned the President for Federal protection

Three Arrested
In McComb Blasts

Clarksdale Press Register, Oct. 1

4th Man Arrested In Bombing

Pascagoula-Moss Point **Chronicle**, Oct. 4

FBI Agents Nab Seven
In McComb Bombings

Starkville News, Oct. 6

McComb Bombers May Get 'Death'

Laurel Leader-Call, Oct. 2

Ten remain in custody under a state law against illegal use of explosives which carries a maximum penalty of death.

One, Sterling L. Gillis, 35, son of a local millionnaire, was free under $5,000 bond.

Natchez Democrat, Oct. 7

Bond is not usually allowed in a capital case, Pigott said, particularly in view of the upcoming grand jury session.

Clarksdale Press Register, Oct. 2

9 Get Suspended Sentences
In McComb Area Bombings

Natchez Democrat, Oct. 24

*Some of those guilty of the McComb bombings were arrested, tried, and given suspended sentences

Text of Judge's Sentence for Bombers

McComb **Enterprise-Journal**, Oct. 28

He told the men they were being treated as they were for three main reasons:

1—They are "mostly young men, just starting out."

2—All came from "good families," who were perhaps "more surprised than anyone else at the implication" of the men in the acts of violence.

3—"You were unduly provoked, and were ill advised."

Circuit Judge W. H. Watkins,
McComb **Enterprise-Journal**,
Oct. 23

Governor Says 'Suspended' Sentences Misunderstood

Jackson **Clarion-Ledger**, Oct. 30

The governor pointed out that the probationary order handed down by Judge Watkins warned the men any further racial violence in the area, whether they were involved or not, could serve to revoke the sentences.

"I certainly believe that these words of Judge Watkins constitute a strong and determined stand against the repetition of the type of action which has occurred in this area," Johnson said.

Starkville News, Oct. 30

"Now, when the law is on your side there's no use and there is no excuse whatever for you doing anything or any act that's contrary to the law, you are both working for the same end, for the same goal, you and the law. But you were not doing it the right way. You should have been cooperating with the law instead of placing your law enforcement officers in jeopardy and in a dangerous situation.

Circuit Judge N. H. Watkins,
McComb **Enterprise Journal**,
Oct. 28

Hoover Cites State Court For Blindness

NEW YORK (UPI) — FBI Director J. Edgar Hoover cited a Mississippi court Saturday as an example of "blindness and indifference to outrageous acts of violence which encourage others to defy the law."

He referred to the court which gave suspended sentences to nine men who were brought to trial following a series of racial bombings.

Delta Democrat-Times, Dec. 13

He said the men were not young, as claimed, but ranged in age from 30 to 44.

J. Edgar Hoover, Director, F.B.I.,
McComb **Enterprise-Journal**,
Nov. 19

Astounding Sentence

We regret that the danger of contempt of court proceedings deters us from saying anything more than that Judge Watkins' judicial action in this instance is more astounding than any other sentences handed down from a Mississippi bench within our memory.

Delta Democrat-Times, Oct. 27

"We should protect our state from invasion and maintain segregation of the races to the full extent that our federal laws will permit, and in the meantime, to live with it peaceably as law-abiding citizens.

"This is no time to panic," he said

Circuit Judge W. H. Watkins,
McComb **Enterprise-Journal**,
Oct. 5

The "bombers" were apprehended, charged, indicted, convicted and sentenced here, although the sentences admittedly were light. This is more than can be said about recent crimes in all areas of Mississippi.

McComb **Enterprise-Journal**,
Oct. 29

Citizens of McComb Assert Responsibility

McComb **Enterprise-Journal.** Nov. 24

Responsible men know that harassment arrests must come to an end.

Responsible men know that we cannot have a dual system of justice—one set of rules to apply to white people and another set of rules for Negro people.

Oliver Emmerich. Editor.
McComb **Enterprise-Journal.**
Oct. 30

Communications can be restored between white and Negro citizens through the mutual recognition that everyone loses when relationships are hostile. But all of us must understand that effective communications cannot be achieved on the basis of the master-servant relationship.

Human dignity is as American as the stars and stripes or the Declaration of Independence.

Human dignity is the core of democratic thinking.

Oliver Emmerich. Editor.
McComb **Enterprise-Journal.**
Oct. 22

Over 600 Sign Statement Here

More than 600 persons today had signed a statement "of principles advocating a responsible" approach to the area's racial troubles.

McComb **Enterprise-Journal,**
Nov. 17

Counter Statement Considered

CIRCULATED at McComb has been an unpublicized counter petition by "Pike Citizens With Honor," with this text:

"We will not pronounce our own dishonor, nor furnish the conclusive evidence of our own self-created degradation, and thereby supply our domestic and foreign news media with a Roman holiday.

"We affirm our belief in law and order, and refute the charge that our law has broken down and that chaotic conditions prevail in our community.

"We cannot commend too highly all of our law enforcement officers, our city officials of McComb, Magnolia, Summit, Osyka, our Board of Supervisors, our Courts and Judges.

"We deny that harassment arrests have been made.

"We oppose any group seeking to speak for the people of Pike County unilaterally on questions of great import which we face today, and not in cooperation with our duly elected officials."

Jackson **Clarion-Ledger,** Nov. 28

A CITIZEN of Pike County —Harry L. Marsalis (306 Fifth St., McComb) — has circulated a public statement suggesting that the McComb Enterprise-Journal, Drew Pearson and certain others have done a "great dis-service to the community."

Following is a direct quote from Mr. Marsalis' statement:

"The editor of the McComb Enterprise-Journal in his editorial of 11-9 speaks about a shot being fired through one of his plate glass windows. I sympathize with the editor's indignation and I would feel the same as he does. I also go along with the editor in what he says, Quote "If efforts of this kind are purposed to frighten our people they can serve no good purpose." The editor has a golden opportunity to take these words, above quoted and shoot them back to Drew Pearson and his other reliable advisers, and tell them that this community will not be frightened or cowered with their threats of economic pressures and that he will not be a source through which they can be disseminated. Will he do it?

I cannot agree that law and order has broken down, the Editor of the Enterprise-Journal and his bosom pal Drew Pearson, to the contrary notwithstanding. I contend the editor of the Enterprise-Journal has rendered a great dis-service to the community he has proclaimed it was a privilege to live in. He has contributed not one mite to the harmony need in our community.

H. L. M.
McComb, Miss.
Jackson **Clarion-Ledger,** Nov. 28

＊**Some of McComb's citizens asserted their responsibility**

CITIZENS FOR PROGRESS

The great majority of our citizens believe in law and order and are against violence of any kind. In spite of this, acts of terrorism have been committed numerous times against citizens both Negro and white.

We believe the time has come for responsible people to speak out for what is right and against what is wrong. For too long we have let the extremists on both sides bring our community close to chaos.

There is only one responsible stance we c a n take: and that is for equal treatment under the law for all citizens regardless of race, creed, position or wealth; for making our protests within the framework of the law; and for obeying the laws of the land regardless of our personal feelings. Certain of these laws may be contrary to our traditions, customs or beliefs, but as God-fearing men a n d women, and as citizens of these United States, we see no other honorable course to follow.

To these ends and for the purpose of restoring peace, tranquility and progress to our area, we respectfully urge the following:

1. Order and respect for law must be reestablished and maintained.

   (a) Law officers should make only lawful arrests. "Harassment" arrests, no matter what the provocation, are not consonant with impartiality of the law.

   (b) To insure the confidence of the people in their officials, we insist that no man is entitled to serve in a public office, elective or appointive, who is a member of any organ-

ization declared to be subversive by the Senate Internal Security Sub-Committee or the United States Army, Navy or Air Force, or to take any obligation upon himself in conflict with his oath of office.

2. Economic threats and sanctions against people of both races must be ended. They only bring harm to both races.

3. We urge citizens of both races to reestablish avenues of communication and understanding. In addition, it is urged that the Negro leadership cooperate with local officials.

4. We urge widest possible use of our citizenship in the selection of juries. We further urge that men called for jury duty not be excused except for the most compelling reasons.

5. We urge our fellow citizens to take a greater interest in public affairs, in the selection of candidates, and in the support and/or constructive criticism of Public Servants.

6. We urge all of our people to approach the future with a renewed dedication and to reflect an attitude of optimism a b o u t o u r county.

We, the undersigned, have read and hereby subscribe and support the principles a n d purposes herein set forth.

(Note: Public officials and public employes have not been asked to sign this petition; some may have voluntarily done so. Anyone who can subscribe to these princip les is invited to do so by contacting any signer.)

Advertisement. McComb **Enterprise-Journal**, Nov. 17

It has been McComb, strangely enough, which has demonstrated what real image building entails. There, a straight-forward statement of support for the law—including the federal law—was adopted.

PRAISE has poured in from all over the nation and all over the world. The McComb Enterprise-Journal has kept its editorial page full with letters from citizens hailing the statement and its results. For once, the national news media has had something good to say about a Mississippi town—not because it was paid to say it, but because something good happened there.

This doesn't mean that the corner has been turned for McComb. There are still plenty of people in Pike County who detest the statement of principles, dislike praise from the outside and are determined to see to it that the status quo is preserved at whatever cost.

Delta Democrat-Times, Nov. 30

Race Riot Not Race Riot If Happens North

Biloxi-Gulfport Herald, July 28

When is a race riot not a race riot? The answer is, when it occurs north of the Potomac. Let one Negro get into an argument over a ham sandwich in Georgia or Mississippi and it is a racial incident. But let hundreds of Negroes pillage and assault in New York, restricting their violence to white people and white - owned property and it is either a "hoodlum mob" or just a bunch of teenagers letting off a bit of steam.

Natchez Democrat, Aug. 24

We wearily call attention once more to the fact that our "roughest" areas are quiet, peaceful valleys when compared to New York.

Columbus Commercial Dispatch, July 27

ARTHUR WINSTEAD, able Mississippi' Congressman, had this to say in a speech on the House floor:

"I shudder to think what would be the fate of the innocent, law-abiding people of Mississippi if the disgraceful New York rioting this past weekend had occurred in my own state.

"Where are the federal marshals that have in the past been sent to Mississippi and Alabama?

It is a sad commentary that while mobs stalk the streets of New York, while innocent women and children are subject to rape, beatings and even murder, some 1,500 so-called civil rights workers and troublemakers are in Mississippi — a state with the nation's lowest crime rate — subjecting innocent, lawabiding people to insult, national scorn and creating trouble wherever these invaders can best serve their own selfish interest.

Jackson Clarion-Ledger, July 23

LOOK AT THIS — Rep. Arthur Winstead of Mississippi yesterday told the House that rioting of Negroes in Harlem shows that civil rights workers in Mississippi should "go home and clean up their own mess." He offers pictures of the New York riots to prove his point. Winstead represents the district which includes Philadelphia, Miss., where three civil rights workers have been missing for several weeks without any trace of their present wherabouts.

—UPI Telephoto

Illinois Man 'Felt Safer' Down South

Pascagoula-Moss Point Chronicle, Sept. 17

A recent report in the Chicago press quotes an Illinois resident as saying he felt "safer in the countryside around Pascagoula where we have often visited than in Chicago, St. Louis, New York."

P. W. K.

Lawrenceville, Illinois

Pascagoula-Moss Point **Chronicle, Sept. 17**

✱ **Mississippians were interested in riots and trouble in other parts of the country**

Latest Wave Of Invaders Badly Needed In New York Area Today

Jackson **Clarion-Ledger**, July 22

Dear Editor:

We suggest that as soon as Mr. Dulles catches his breath and while bags are still packed he rush to Chicago for investigation of and report on law enforcement problems. Also suggest he swing by New York on way back, if he can spare time from Southern duties, for similar evaluations there,

Is it possible that "beefed up" F.B.I. units might be of assistance?

Reports circulated here are that murders in areas outside the South are of much lesser importance than those below the "Smith and Wesson" line. But there is also some doubt locally and fear is growing rapidly, that those murdered in other areas possibly are as dead as those treated similarly here.

Signed: Southerners united for preservation of Chicago and New York.
By R. L. G., Secy.
Jackson
Jackson **Clarion-Ledger**, July 1

Dear Editor:

Demonstrators break the law promiscuously and then, in the same breath cry and bleat like a billy goat getting his throat cut, for protection, protection. So what can you expect when high officials are bowing to these minority groups, pressure groups condoning pure naked lawlessness.

So far it is reasonably safe for our people to walk the streets after dark and we aim to keep it that way. However, it is not safe after dark in other places such as New York, Chicago, Californa, Maryland and many other such places which are the very spawning grounds of these dirty filthy, Godless "No Gooders" preying on us.

(Name withheld) **Meridian Star,**
July 25

MERIDIAN STAR:

Our vacation will consist of "making a run for it" to New Jersey, spending a hurried vacation and rushing back to the safety of the Deep South. Also, my Aunt told us she would give us a New York license plate to use while there. We plan to remove our Mississippi tag and, drive with a "lost tag" sign for fear of damage of person or property. She said that she would have to screen our conversationalists while there. A sad time indeed when one fears reprisals in a FREE country!

J. J., age 14
Meridian, Miss.

Meridian Star, July 1

THE LURID, leftist Saturday Evening Post has just come out with another vicious smear of Mississippi as a hotbed of violence — at the very moment race riots are raging in New York while peace reigns in our own state.

This Post article, "If We Can Crack Mississippi," glorifies the beatnik - weirdo students and their Communist - infiltrated projects. It low - rates our state and people as bigots, rednecks, & etc.

In other words, it's the same old hogwash characteristic of Post reporting on Mississippi matters.

Jackson **Clarion-Ledger**, July 23

Dear Editor:

What a distorted sense of balance rules the oddballs in our nation's capitol!

Washington, D.C. is so rotten with crime it is the laughing stock of the world. New York City is so ungodly, Christian leaders there have asked that services be held only during daylight hours.

Yet, and yet, Mississippi, with the second lowest crime record in the fifty states, is now ringed with FBI and hordes of

Dear Editor:

The President of the United States, Mr. "Lightning Bug" Johnson, has stated that he has ordered the Federal Bureau of Investigation to investigate the riots which are plaguing our great America, in order to see if there is a pattern regarding these riots throughout our land.

We as Americans know that the Communists have instigated these terrible acts and are using the Negroes as a tool to accomplish their goal. Why would it take the President this long in ordering such an investigation?

On the other hand, when one Negro Church happens to burn, he does not wait but instantly orders hundreds of F.B.I. men into the sovereign State of Mississippi.

We believe that there is definitely a pattern of the bombings, but do not believe that it is coming from the white radicals as many of the liberals, socialists, Communists, and the news media and many of our crooked politicians have stated.

For instance, in the historic city of Natchez, Miss., on August 14, 1964, a juke joint was bombed and burned and it was stated that it was the act of the white radicals, but as we later found out, a Negro man had willfully, unlawfully and felonously attempted to set fire to another place of business owned by the same man on August 13, 1964, the day before the bombing took place but no arrest was made at that time. Therefore, on August 13, this man attempted to commit an act similar to the one on August 14. How long will the white man be persecuted?

E. L. McDaniel, Grand Dragon of the United Klans of America, Knights of Ku Klux Klan, Realm of Mississippi,
Jackson **Clarion-Ledger**,
Sept. 30

student slime, sanctioned by both the guys in Washington who cannot clean up around their own doorsteps, and that scummy bunch of reds operating under the guise of church! Why, even one self-appointed "Negro Saviour" sponsored by the latter said he did not even believe in God!

An American Patriot
Laurel
Jackson **Clarion-Ledger**, July 20

131

COURT ORDERS SCHOOLS

Public school officials at Jackson, Biloxi and in Leake County prepared for desegregation of the systems facilities in the wake of a permanent order by U.S. Dist. Judge Sidney Mize ordering the schools desegregated in the fall.

In his decision, Mize said differences between the races in learning capacities "cry out" for a re-evaluation of the U.S. Supreme Court's 1954 decision.

Vicksburg Post, July 9

Carry On The Fight

The horrors of school integration are upon us with a vengeance.

On Monday in Biloxi, Negroes and Whites will be forced to attend school together below the college level, for the first time in our state.

The Carthage and Jackson schools are scheduled to be forced to do likewise.

We can find no words to adequately express our shock — our revulsion at this abominable crime of race mixing.

Meridian Star, Aug. 26

Only One Negro Child Enrolled At Carthage

West Point **Times Leader,** Sept. 2

UGLY DUCKLING?

A lot of folks have been wondering how our white school teachers are going to feel with speckled student bodies? But, the real question may rest with the Negro teachers. If integration is inevitable . . . they are in for a tough squeeze when white teachers are, as in the North, found preferable.

Jackson Clarion-Ledger, Aug. 22

UPI

Only 17 Negroes sign up at Biloxi

Hattiesburg American, Aug. 15

Clarksdale School Integration Fizzles; No Negroes Sign Up

Corinth **Corinthian,** Aug. 25

Says Fear Stymies School Integration

Corinth **Corinthian,** Oct. 7

＊ Public schools: another problem for Mississippi

132

TO BEGIN MIXING

Columbus **Commercial Dispatch**, July 30

Police officers stood guard while first graders in eight of 26 Jackson, Miss., schools were integrated

Negro School Refuse White

CLARKSDALE, Miss. (AP) —The principal of a Negro elementary school turned away a white first grader who attempted to register today because the youngster lacked a birth certificate.

It was the first bi-racial attempt to cross previous color lines in first grade registration here under a federal court desegregation order.

Later, a parent of the white pupil called the principal and withdrew the child's application.

McComb Enterprise-Journal, Aug. 24

43 Negroes Are Registered At White Jackson Schools

Corinth **Corinthian**, Aug. 24

Cops Only Difference In Jackson Schools

Tupelo **Journal**, Aug. 21

Negroes Rejected At Jackson High Schools

West Point **Times Leader**, Sept. 10

School Segregation By Sex Asked By Governor Johnson

Meridian Star, July 8

The Mississippi House of Representatives has passed a bill separating the sexes in public schools . . . upon necessity.

Rep. Frank Shanahan and the numerous legislators who co-signed the act, readily admit that the bill is a wee bit repugnant to them, but situations may arise which will make such bars necessary.

Health, morals and education are set forth as prime reasons for the bill.

Remember the girl in the desk behind who platted the long hair on your sleepy head so many years ago? . . . She'll be missed.

Jackson Clarion-Ledger, July 16

The governor said Mississippians are to be congratulated for acting the opposite to the way others thought they would.

He called upon leaders to use their brains rather than their vocal chords . . . to look at the main goals for the future.

Natchez Democrat, Aug. 11

Warning Against Sex Offenders Is Issued

Tupelo Journal, Sept. 4

TUPELO, Miss. (AP) — Tupelo Mayor James Ballard said today 10,000 pamphlets dealing with the problem of sexual deviates will be mailed to Tupelo school students and their parents.

The pamphlets outline the menace of sexual deviates and how to cope with them.

Ballard said many of the pamphlets will be distributed to adult Sunday School classes, as well as throughout the city school system.

Biloxi-Gulfport **Herald**, Sept. 3

Many Schools Not Accredited

JACKSON, Miss. — If accreditation of high schools by the Southern Association of Colleges and Schools is a good measure of quality education, Mississippians may be a little startled over the status of accredited schools in the state.

Records in the state department of education showed last week that of the 187 Negro high schools in the state, only 15, including the two new ones, have been accredited by the Southern Association. At the same time the records showed that of the 338 white high schools 100 were on the accredited list.

The association decreed that a minimum salary of $3,600 for teachers will be required in order to meet the basic standards for approval.

The Mississippi salary schedule provides $3,300 for beginning BA degree teachers, graduated up to $3,900 with six years experience.

This makes it obvious that local schools will have to supplement teachers' salaries above the state's contribution to become accredited.

McComb Enterprise-Journal, Dec. 9

Dr. Kirby Walker, superintendent of Jackson schools, testified in the suit that schools are segregated in the best interest of both white and Negro students.

Jackson Daily News, July 7

He said he found no evidence to show injury to Negroes from separate schools nor did he find any advantage in "mixed schools."

U.S. District Judge Sidney Mize, Jackson Daily News, July 7

"I find they (the Negroes) are very, very happy. They are happy because of the money spent on education in Mississippi — 59 cents of every tax dollar."

Governor Paul Johnson, Grenada Sentinel-Star, Nov. 30

We Dare Not Rear Generation Of Cripples

If we begin to slip backward even a little at a time when the rest of America is planning an unprecedented educational surge forward, we will not merely cripple Mississippi's economy but will cripple her people in a way that will be extremely difficult and costly to overcome in the later years of their lives.

As Mississippi enters the age of space there are in our state approximately 640,000 adults with less than a high school education.

That is roughly three-fifths of all the men and women in our state.

And contrary to popular opinion 250,000 of these adults who failed to finish high school are whites.

Tupelo **Journal**, July 2

Private Tuition Grants Approved By Legislature

Tupelo **Journal**, July 30

Special Session Costs Taxpayers Nearly $180,000

Tupelo **Journal**, July 16

Johnson Praises Special Session Action

Tupelo **Journal**, July 17

A bill was introduced in the Senate, that would appropriate $1 million to implement the private education plan, to be administered by the State Educational Finance Commission.

A number of leaders indicated they felt the state should borrow funds to start the program rather than vote any new appropriation requiring increased revenue.

Pascagoula-Moss Point **Chronicle, July 1**

SINCE last winter, the state has been borrowing heavily — at the rate of as much as $10 million per month — to keep itself solvent, and quite often about the only money the state has are funds that it has borrowed. We are, in fact, perenially just one step ahead of the bill collector.

Delta Democrat-Times, July 11

Alcorn County teachers won't be getting salaries

CORINTH, Miss. (AP) — School Supt. Bobby R. DePoyster has told teachers from Biggersville and Kossuth the Alcorn County School Board is broke and their salaries—amounting to $12,000—will not be paid Friday.

DePoyster said a request to borrow $30,000 to pay salaries and meet other board obligations has been ignored by the county board of supervisors.

Hattiesburg American, July 30

* "Mississippians for Public Education" made themselves felt while the governor segregated the schools by sex and called a special legislative session to consider tuition grants for private schooling

No Borrowing Planned To Pay Teacher Wages

Jackson **Clarion-Ledger, Dec. 5**

Gov. Paul B. Johnson said here late Friday that he has no intention of borrowing $4,000,-000 to finance a payment of teachers' salaries.

Much has been written the past several days of a shortage of funds to meet current bills. It was reported that while a payment of more than $6,000,-000 was due the teachers, only approximately $2,000,000 reposed in the general fund to meet the bill.

Jackson **Clarion-Ledger, Dec. 8**

First Thing We Saw Was A 'The Nigger Was Lying Kind

"The first thing we saw was a shoe."

The shoe was on the foot of Andrew Goodman, a young New Yorker who had come to Mississippi to save its Negroes from segregation. The man who saw the shoe protruding from the red clay of a small pond dam was a Mississippi construction worker.

He had dug straight down through 14 feet of dirt to the bodies of Michael Schwerner, Goodman and Meridian Negro James Chaney. The trio was the civil rights workers missing from the Philadelphia area since June 21.

"The nigger was lying kind of on top of the two white men. The bulldozer ran over him. He was laying at the feet of the two white men, who were laying head to head. The white men had shoes on; the nigger was barefooted."

"No, we didn't dig anywhere else. Heck, they knew where we were supposed to dig."

Did he ever see any highway patrolmen or other state officers?

"Man, they wouldn't let any highway patrolmen in there. They wouldn't let in any deputies or constables, either. I don't know who all the men were. I know John Proctor (resident FBI agent at Meridian). He was in charge."

"There were about 150 FBI agents there."

"The next time I go on a job they're going to have to tell me where I'm going and what I'm going to do.

"I wouldn't do that again."

Meridian Star, Sept. 20

EDITORIALS:

Cause For Optimism

A new hate campaign against Mississippi is sure to follow the finding of the bodies of three civil rights workers near Philadelphia.

We know that, no matter who the murderers are, the "civil rights" organizations share the blame, inasmuch as they care nothing for how much violence they provoke.

The "liberals" won't give us a fair shake no matter what. We are used to this. We have been a whipping boy for years.

Nevertheless, we can take great consolation from what we ourselves know to be the truth, regardless of the foul lies that others tell.

Furthermore, we know that more and more people in other parts of the country are coming to understand and sympathize with our cause.

Truly, in spite of everything, we have good reason to be optimistic.

Meridian Star, Aug. 6

Philadelphians React but Slightly to News

Most persons declined to talk, and even in the local cafes the businessmen seemed to avoid the subject on purpose.

Meridian Star, Aug. 6

One farmer stopped on a downtown street told a reporter yesterday: "I think it was those integration groups that got rid of them. They couldn't let them live after they disappeared for fear everyone would find out it was a hoax."

Meridian Star, Aug. 6

Another man, who also refused to give his name, said "if they had stayed home where they belonged nothing would have happened to them."

Hattiesburg American, Aug. 5

McComb Enterprise-Journal, Aug. 5

"It proves to me that we have people in Mississippi that will destroy a person, not because of his color, but because of what the person stands for."

Natchez Democrat, Aug. 8

Winstead said "no one can condone murder and violence, but folks have been killed in other sections of the country in racial outbreaks.

"And when people from one section of the country go into another section looking for trouble, they usually find it."

McComb Enterprise-Journal, Aug. 6

Foot,' Dam Digger Says, Of On Top Of White Men'

Meridian Star, Sept. 20

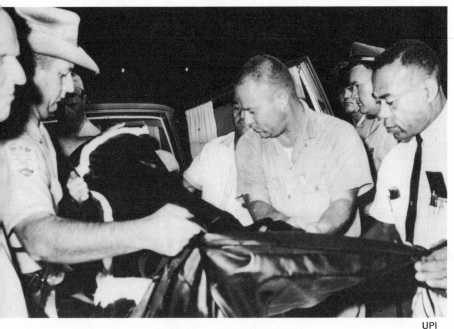

UPI

ARRIVE FOR AUTOPSY — Bodies of the three missing civil rights workers were brought to the University Medical Center in Jackson early Wednesday morning for an autopsy. Officers are shown removing one of the bodies from an ambulance which brought them from Philadelphia. Officer in hat, at left, is Neshoba Deputy Sheriff Cecil Price, who had arrested the trio on a speeding charge shortly before they disappeared.

Jackson **Clarion-Ledger**, Aug. 6

Property Owner Has No Idea How Three Bodies Buried There

Corinth **Corinthian**, Aug. 5

PHILADELPHIA, Miss. (UPI)—Olen Burrage, 42, said today he had no idea who placed the bodies of three civil rights workers in a grave on his property near this East Mississippi town.

"I tell you I just don't know anybody that would kill them and put them on my property," Burrage said.

West Point **Times Leader**, Aug. 5

MERIDIAN (UPI)— Thumbnail profiles of the 21 white Mississippians charged in connection with the June, 1964, slayings of three civil rights workers near Philadelphia, Miss.:

OLEN L. Burrage, 34, owner of Burrage Trucking Company, Philadelphia; married, two children. He owns the farm where the bodies were found

Delta Democrat-Times, Dec. 6

✱ Forty-four days later the bodies of the vanished civil rights workers were found on "Old Jolly Farm" just outside Philadelphia, Miss.

Philadelphia Asks Only A 'Fair Shake' From All

Meridian Star, July 8

"Great progress" is being made, Hoover said, in solving the slaying of three civil rights workers near Philadelphia, Miss.

But, he said, "around Philadelphia, Miss., law enforcement is practically nil and many times sheriffs and deputies participate in crime."

J. Edgar Hoover, Director, F.B.I., McComb Enterprise-Journal, Nov. 19

In Philadelphia, Sheriff Lawrence Rainey said Saturday he was offered money by FBI agents for information about the slayings Rainey said agents told him they had witnesses.

The FBI declined comment on the witness but said the money claim was "ridiculous."

McComb Enterprise-Journal. Dec. 17

The poison pen sweepings of the gutters of journalism go on printing their lying trash about their eminently decent fellow Americans in Philadelphia.

The coffers of COFO go on getting fatter and fatter and its officials go on riding higher and higher.

Meridian Star, July 12

Steve Schapiro

Philadelphia police officers

✱ **Philadelphia, Miss., and Neshoba county did not want to be misunderstood**

Now there is going to be another opportunity for justice in Neshoba County. The three civil rights workers did not kill themselves, then carefully dig their way into an unfinished dam and hide for more than a month. Someone murdered them, and it is a safe bet that the FBI will in the near future make an arrest.

Delta Democrat-Times, Aug. 9

Neshoba Sheriff Gets Case Of Red Man

Meridian Star, Sept. 16

Lawrence Rainey, sheriff of Philadelphia

PHILADELPHIA —

Sheriff Lawrence Rainey of Neshoba County had received a gift of Red Man chewing tobacco from the Pinkerton Tobacco Co., Toledo, Ohio.

The letter which accompanied the gift of chewing tobacco to Sheriff Rainey follows.

"We saw your picture in the September 5 issue of the Saturday Evening Post and in our opinion, it was a beautiful picture.

"We appreciate the extreme lower right hand corner which showed a part of a package of Red Man Chewing Tobacco. We also appreciate the man-size chew which you carried in your right cheek. The mention of the Red Man Chewing Tobacco in the article made us very happy too.

"We are sending you under separate cover and with o u r compliments, two dozen Red Man regular size for y o u r chewing pleasure. If you wish, you may keep one dozen in your office and one dozen in the new tan Oldsmobile with the powerful red light on top that is filled with guns, nightsticks and extra cartons of Red Man.

"We appreciate all our customers, signed L. R. Jump, sales manager."

Jackson Clarion-Ledger, Sept. 16

While the two FBI agents were waiting, Rainey was conferring with a newsman in his office. When the door opened and Rainey came out with the newsman, the two agents walked around the corner and said: "May we have five minutes with you?"

Said Rainey: "Have you got a warrant?"

Murtaugh, a prematurely silverhaired agent replied: "No."

"Then come see me when you have one and I'll be glad to talk to you then." Rainey said.

"You're not going to cooperate with the FBI?

"As much as the FBI cooperates with me," Rainey replied.

Meridian Star, Aug. 10

Sheriff Refuses Talk FBI
Natchez Democrat, Aug. 11

Sheriff Wants Warrant Before Talking To FBI
Laurel Leader-Call, Aug. 11

No Telephone Call For Warrants, Neshoba's County Attorney Says
Meridian Star, Aug. 11

*FBI agents had problems in the community

139

Ted Polumbaum

Mrs. Michael Schwerner, widow of one of the three civil rights workers

Thousands gather at services for workers

Meridian Star, Aug. 10

CORE

Andrew Goodman

James Chaney

Michael Schwerner

Now that the three missing civil rights workers have been found, brutally murdered, in Neshoba County, many of us in Mississippi need to take a long hard look at ourselves.

We could begin by altering the sorry record of interracial justice which we have made over the past decade. In celebrated case after case involving the murders of Negroes, from Emmet Till through Medgar Evers, we have been seemingly unable or unwilling to find the guilty parties, try and convict them. The roll call of the dead is long. The list of those convicted is still a blank page.

Let us pray that this time, if the evidence is clear, a jury will find it in themselves to convict. It is irrelevant what passions stirred the men who shot down the three young men. What is relevant is that justice must prevail.

Delta Democrat-Times, Aug. 9

* The nation mourned

FBI NAMES 21 IN CR SLAYING

Laurel Leader-Call, Dec. 4

Commissioner releases 20 in 'workers' hearing

Grenada Sentinel-Star, Dec. 11

MERIDIAN, Miss. (UPI) —A U. S. commissioner conducting a preliminary hearing today blocked testimony concerning an alleged confession which the FBI says it has from one of the 21 men charged in connection with the slaying of three civil rights workers.

The purpose of the preliminary hearing conducted by U.S. Commissioner Esther Carter, was to determine whether the charges should be continued against the suspects. Only 19 of the 21 defendants were involved in today's hearing.

Miss Carter refused to allow FBI agent Henry Rask to testify about an alleged confession which he took from Horace Doyle Barnette, 22, one of the defendants.

The commissioner said she based her ruling on the fact that it was hearsay because Barnette himself was not in the U. S. District courtroom for the hearing.

Grenada Sentinel-Star, Dec. 10

The Justice Department complained it was the first time in memory heresay evidence was ruled out at a preliminary hearing.

Delta Democrat-Times, Dec. 13

At a memorial service later, Dave Dennis, assistant program director of the Mississippi "Summer Project," recalled several previous cases in which Negroes were lynched or slain.

"I remember what has happened to the people who did these things," he told the some 700 in the audience. "Nothing."

Memorial Service for James Chaney, Slain civil rights worker, Laurel Leader-Call, Aug. 8

* Mississippi justice

Our Purpose Must Be Unmistakably Clear

We have a job to do, and our purpose in doing that job must be unmistakably clear. We must track down the murderers of these men, and we must bring them to justice.

Vicksburg Post, Aug. 6

Lowest Crime Rate Belongs To Mississippi

Paradoxically the report showed that Mississippians murder each other at a rate far exceeding many major cities around the nation.

F.B.I. Annual Report, 1963,
Meridian Star, July 21

It is sometimes difficult to tell whether you are close to the situation or far away, but the attitude in Mississippi about the proper way to meet the problems posed by desegregation is slowly but perceptibly beginning to alter for the better. Where once there was monolithic unanimity, cloaked always in the terms of unyielding resistance, there are today indications in several quarters that lawful acceptance of the inevitable changes is becoming a tenable, but still not popular, position in the white community.

Delta Democrat-Times, July 21

Two Men Freed In Torso Deaths

Jackson **Daily News,** Jan. 11

City Park, Canton, Miss.

Kenneth Thompson, NCC

Mississippi Image

Pascagoula-Moss Point
Chronicle, Nov. 25